You Can't
Get Rid Of Me

"To all my brothers and sisters, both biological and chosen. Hang in there. We are all survivors."

PRAISE FOR: *YOU CAN'T GET RID OF ME*

This impressive first book effortlessly dances across time, beginning with the opening scene of Scott hunched over the computer, studying Ancestry.com. Despite growing up in a strict home while wrestling with his own queer identity and braving time in a mental hospital, sex work, and addiction, Scott never wavers. His courage to continue his quest for belonging is the beam of inspiration that makes this memoir intimate, comforting, and thought-provoking.

— *Abby McCabe, Booklist*

You Can't Get Rid of Me is one of the most honest, raw, and beautifully told stories I've read in a long time. As a friend and journalist, I'm so proud to see the way Jesse doesn't hold anything back, and what unfolds as a result is a journey full of pain, humor, survival, and ultimately, self-acceptance. Growing up gay in the '70s, navigating adoption, institutions, and identity - this book is more than a memoir, it's a testament to what it means to fight for who you are. I laughed, cried, and rooted for him every step of the way. This book will stay with you.

—*Bianca Rae, Journalist*

"You Can't Get Rid of Me" is simply a remarkable story about survival, resiliency, forgiveness and acceptance. This is the true story of Jesse Scott, a now 60-something gay man who tells his life story with brutal raw honesty and a sharp sense of humor. Adopted by a conservative "Leave it To Beaver"esque family in the late 50s, Jesse tells the incredible story of coming out when he was only 12 years old and consequently being committed to a mental hospital in 1970 where his fellow inmates were mostly adults. I couldn't help but picture Jesse as an unlikely character in "One Flew Over the Cuckoo's Nest."

This book has so many twists and turns that often it doesn't feel like it is real, but it is and it is marvelous. From drug addiction, a jail sentence, living with HIV, finding the love of his life and eventually finding his bio mother and a whole new slew of relatives, Jesse's story is one of hope, humor, love against all odds and the ability to find the silver lining always.

—*Rachel O'Sullivan, retired military journalist, mixed media artist and avid reader*

From foster homes to found families, from heartbreak to healing, Jesse Scott's story is a courageous embrace of life's toughest roads. In this unflinching and deeply human memoir, Scott invites readers into the raw truth of his journey—navigating the child welfare system, searching for belonging, and ultimately discovering the strength within to not only survive, but to thrive.

With honesty, grit, and unexpected moments of grace, *You Can't Get Rid of Me* is more than a story of endurance—it's a testament to the resilience of the human spirit and the power of never giving up.

Jesse Scott reminds the reader that the human spirit is stronger than many imagine. He reminds us to never give up, believe in yourself, and pursue what makes you whole.

—David Brinkman

...A captivating memoir that captures the essence of resilience, identity, and the pursuit of acceptance. This vivid narrative takes readers through the tumultuous journey of growing up LGBTQ in the 1970s—a time when not conforming to societal norms presented significant challenges. The inclusion of historical context enriches the narrative, giving readers insight into the era and the social dynamics that shaped Jesse's life. This memoir reflects the ongoing challenges faced by the LGBTQ community, making it a relevant read even today.

Jesse Scott and Keri Ault brilliantly capture Jesse's experiences, balancing humorous anecdotes with deeply poignant moments that will resonate with anyone who has ever felt marginalized. A significant moment occurs when Jesse and Lee wear their mother's diamond earrings at her funeral, symbolizing their ongoing connection and shared grief. Each wearing one earring illustrates a mutual support system, sharing the weight of their loss equally and reinforcing their bond as they navigate the mourning process. The choice of diamond earrings symbolizes the lasting and unbreakable nature of their love and memory of their mother. Diamonds, known for their toughness and endurance, represent the strength of the family ties and the lasting impact of their mother's life, which sums up the book concisely. Scott and Ault have created a memoir that celebrates the courage it takes to live authentically, making *You Can't Get Rid of Me* an inspiring read.

—Carol Thompson, *Readers' Favorite*

Jesse's story is a powerful reminder of the importance of family, connection, relationship and identity.

—Toni Ferguson, *Adoptive parent and former case manager*

The feeling of being accepted is truly explored in this book. Jesse Scott's use of imagery and raw honesty elevates the narrative, stirring up powerful emotions ranging from anger and fear to a longing for hope and closure. *You Can't Get Rid of Me* is a beautiful story with lifelong lessons on family, love, and acceptance.

—Adanna Ora, *Readers' Favorite*

You Can't Get Rid Of Me

**JESSE SCOTT
& KERI AULT**

Anamcara Press LLC

Published in 2025 by Anamcara Press LLC
Author © 2025 by Jesse Scott and Keri Ault
Cover photograph: Jesse Scott 1970
Adobe Caslon Pro, Pulpo Rust, Berlin Sans FB
Printed in the United States of America.

Book Description: You will laugh and you will cry, but you won't be able to put down *You Can't Get Rid Of Me*, an unflinching reveal of growing up LGBTQ in the 1970s, and a quest for belonging.

ANAMCARA PRESS LLC
P.O. Box 442072, Lawrence, KS 66044
https://anamcara-press.com/

Ordering Information:
Quantity sales. Special discounts are available on quantity purchases by corporations, associations, and others. For details, contact the publisher at the address above.
Orders by U.S. trade bookstores and wholesalers. Please contact Ingram Distribution.
ISBN-13: 978-1-960462-60-2 eBook
ISBN-13: 978-1-960462-59-6 paperback

BIO031000   BIOGRAPHY & AUTOBIOGRAPHY / LGBTQ+
FAM058000   FAMILY & RELATIONSHIPS / Family History & Genealogy
FAM004000   FAMILY & RELATIONSHIPS / Adoption & Fostering
FAM052000   FAMILY & RELATIONSHIPS / Dysfunctional Families
BIO026000   BIOGRAPHY & AUTOBIOGRAPHY / Memoirs

Library of Congress Control Number: 2024950611

"An individual having unusual difficulties in coping with his environment struggles and kicks up the dust, as it were. I have used the figure of a fish caught on a hook; his gyrations must look peculiar to the other fish that don't understand his circumstances; but his splashes are not his affliction, they are his effort to get rid of his affliction and every fisherman knows these efforts may succeed."
—Dr. Karl Menninger, from "Asylum to Action," by Helen Spandler, 2006.

"I don't take myself too seriously; life's too short for that."
—Liberace

Jesse Scott 1977

CONTENTS

Forward

Northern California, 1879

Adelia's hands were shaking as she struggled to set her oar in the water off the side of the canoe, and push off the muddy shore of the Trinity river. The shaking was spreading through her body and her senses were on fire. She scanned the shore for any sign of movement. She knew the ways of the animals in this section of water, but it was the white men she was terrified of seeing emerge through the thick bushes and trees. Adelia's hands slipped off the oar and as she looked down she realized they were covered in blood. White man's blood. Her eyes continued to dart around as she wiped first the right and then the left hand on the tatters of her torn dress.

Adelia's mind was spinning. Things happened so fast. She had been in the woods, gathering berries in the thick bushes, filling her bucket. She had set a line for fish and was hoping to bring back a couple of salmon for dinner. She had been humming one of the songs her sister had been singing lately. Her mind wasn't on anything in particular, but she remembered the feeling of the hairs rising on the back of her neck when she first heard the brush crack in the way that wasn't animal.

He was standing there, watching her. Smoking a cigarette. Staring. He didn't say anything and she didn't know what to do. She had seen the white men before, the ones with the uniforms from the Fort nearby. Calvary, she thought they were called. Someone said that was a fancy term that meant they rode horses, but different horses than the ones on the reservation. Their men didn't need to have a fancy name just to say they rode horses. Rumor was her daddy was white, but she didn't know if he was a soldier. Her mama, Hoopa Sally, didn't talk about him much.

The man didn't say anything, but the way he stared at her, she didn't want to stick around. Wild animals didn't respond well to sudden movements, or to fear, so she slowly continued to pick berries as she made her way down the river, carrying her bag on her shoulder. She noticed she stopped humming, and she heard the man taking steps in her direction.

Adelia turned around just as he grabbed her by the hair with one hand and pinned her arm against her side with the other. She smelled alcohol and smoke and sweat and could hear him grunting as he struggled to get control of her. Adelia dropped the berries and began to claw at his face but the man was strong and suddenly she felt the thud of her head on the ground. Pain seared through her head as the man pinned her down with his legs. He kept grunting as he covered her mouth with one hand and began unbuckling his belt with the other. Adelia tried to bite down but she could hardly breathe, much less inflict pain. He was pawing and tearing and now he was thrusting and the pain in her head was replaced by an excruciating ripping deep inside where Adelia didn't know could hurt this much.

She looked past the man's hideous face and focused on a hawk that was perched high in the redwood tree. Adelia knew these woods and she had seen this bird before. The nest was close by, but the hawk seemed to be watching her, watching this scene. The soldier seemed so focused on the thrusting, it was as if Adelia wasn't even there. Tears ran down her face as she stayed focused on the bird. The soldier's grunts became faster and Adelia's right hand felt the cloth of her bag. He didn't seem to notice her small movements, and she looked at the hawk as her hand felt inside the bag. She finally felt the wooden handle of the bowie knife she had used earlier to clear some brush for better berries. The knife she was planning to use to filet the fish. The man let out a loud moan and then collapsed on top of her, his weight smothering her. He was quiet, and then he rolled off, pants down around his ankles, a look of smug satisfaction on his face.

Adelia grasped the knife firmly as she sprang up and over the soldier. The knife entered the top of his groin and she pulled up, toward his heart, his flesh ripping open efficiently, through skin and fat and then organs. The soldier's eyes widened and he gasped as blood gushed out of his abdomen, intestines spilling out as he tried to move to grab her. Adelia had gutted rabbits, deer, and once a bear. This was similar, but different. There were clothes instead of fur. Adelia looked him in the eye and made sure he was dead before she dropped the knife and took off running. Toward the canoe. Toward the reservation.

Adelia found a rhythm as the oar sliced through the river. She was shaking and fighting the urge to vomit into the river. She looked up into the trees and found the hawk. He had flown to a tree down river and seemed to be following her toward the Hoopa reservation. Toward her people. Her breath began to even out and the shaking started to settle down. A numbness took over and her thoughts began to settle back into her body. Adelia knew she would never be able to leave the reservation again, but she would be safe there. Protected. The hawk flew down the river to another tree. Waiting for her. Bringing her home.

John, Jesse and Les on vacation at resort in Mazatlan, Mexico 2014

Chapter 1

Palm Springs, 2016

It's another blazing hot day in Palm Springs and the air conditioning is blasting, but I am still sweating. It's not like I'm hot, necessarily; it's a nervous sweat. The kind that I get when I'm around people. Well, not all people, because most people who know me know I'm a total extrovert. It's more like the way I sweat when I'm around people that I want to impress, or who I think might reject me or something. It's almost like the kind of sweat I used to get when I was paranoid from tweaking. Even though I haven't been a tweaker for years, that feeling comes up sometimes, which really doesn't seem fair. But I got over things being fair a long, long, time ago.

I've been on the computer looking at this site, Ancestry.com. It's one of those sites where people go on to look at their past, to see if they were related to royalty or celebrities or something. To find their heritage or what country they came from. It's a pretty straightforward name. I suppose, for most people it works like that, straightforward. Plug in your information and it spits out your heritage. Easy Peasy. Like most things in my life, it doesn't work that way. Ever since me and my brother were put up for adoption, a million years ago, *straightforward* just doesn't seem to apply. Good, bad, messed up. We've gone through all of it, and sometimes all in the same day.

There's my phone buzzing. John is texting me telling me to change out the load of laundry and take the chicken out of the freezer for tonight's dinner. "And get your butt off the computer," he tells me. This is how I know I'm not really paranoid. In my paranoid days I would think he could actually see me and I would spend time looking all over the house for cameras. Now I know that he just knows me well enough to know I spend a lot of time on the computer on my days off. Especially while I look at this site.

John is off at his job slicing fancy meats for the fancy people. He has no interest in things like ancestry. He knows his family, and even though his parents died when he was young, he's pretty close to his brother and sister. Well, he's *close*, but he still refers to me as his roommate. I don't know how stupid he thinks they are, but he likes to keep a *Don't Ask Don't Tell* attitude about his being gay. The way I see it, if you have the same roommate for years and you live in Palm Springs and your jeans have rhinestones on the pockets, well, I think we're beyond "don't tell." I try not to push it. After 17 years together, he considers me family too, just not enough to tell his siblings we're in love.

I need a cigarette. We've been forcing ourselves to go outside to smoke even though it's 104 degrees out there right now. We think it will make us cut down, which is a good idea. I've been cheating though, standing in the doorway while my cigarette hand is outside. There's a little lemon tree outside that gives off some shade. If I stand under there, I can pretend that it's not so hot. At least this produces real sweat. And real relief, even though I know breathing in cancer-air isn't good for me.

Thank God Les is gone and I don't have to sit out here with him or pick up his underwear around the house. He was just here for his annual 6-week stay in Palm Springs. John and I try to make the best of it when he's here because we don't really have any choice in the matter. Technically, this is his house even though he told me he bought it for me, and it's in my name.

Les is in his 80s and still manages to drive down from the Oregon Coast a few times a year. I first met him when I was an 18-year-old prostitute on the streets of Portland and he was a 40-year-old trick of mine that just kept coming back. Poor guy fell in love with me, and has been my Sugar Daddy ever since. John calls him "Lester the Molester" and when the two of them first met it was ugly, especially when alcohol was involved. There was already tension, and sometimes a little drink would help everyone relax. Several drinks, on the other hand, would bring out the ugliness.

At first, I tried to be the mediator, but I also realized that they were two grown men, so I would just go to bed and assume they wouldn't kill each other in the night. They both agreed to a type of truce, tolerating each other as best they could. Les appreciated John's cooking, and he knew John made me happy. John appreciated getting to go on vacation to Les's timeshares, and he knew that if Les hadn't bought me this house, he would be paying a lot more in rent. I knew Les wouldn't be around forever, and in some ways he's my family, too.

Maybe I am being harsh about Les. Even though we met under circumstances that were not ideal, he has really been there for me. There were times when my own parents cut me off financially but I could still count on Les to send me cash to get me out of a bad spot.

I would come up with all kinds of cock-and-bull stories about why I needed money—*but not for drugs*—because Les hated that I used drugs, and he would send me money.

Granted, I would usually use that money to buy drugs, which I guess some could say was enabling of him. I knew he hated it, though. He would tell me he knew I could be doing something better with my life. It was like he believed in me.

I have told Les things I haven't been able to tell other

people and he never left. Again, I'm not saying that he's not a bit of a pervert, but he's *my* pervert. We haven't had sex in decades, so I should probably stop referring to him as my Sugar Daddy. Old habits die hard though, I remind myself, as I take the last drag of my cigarette.

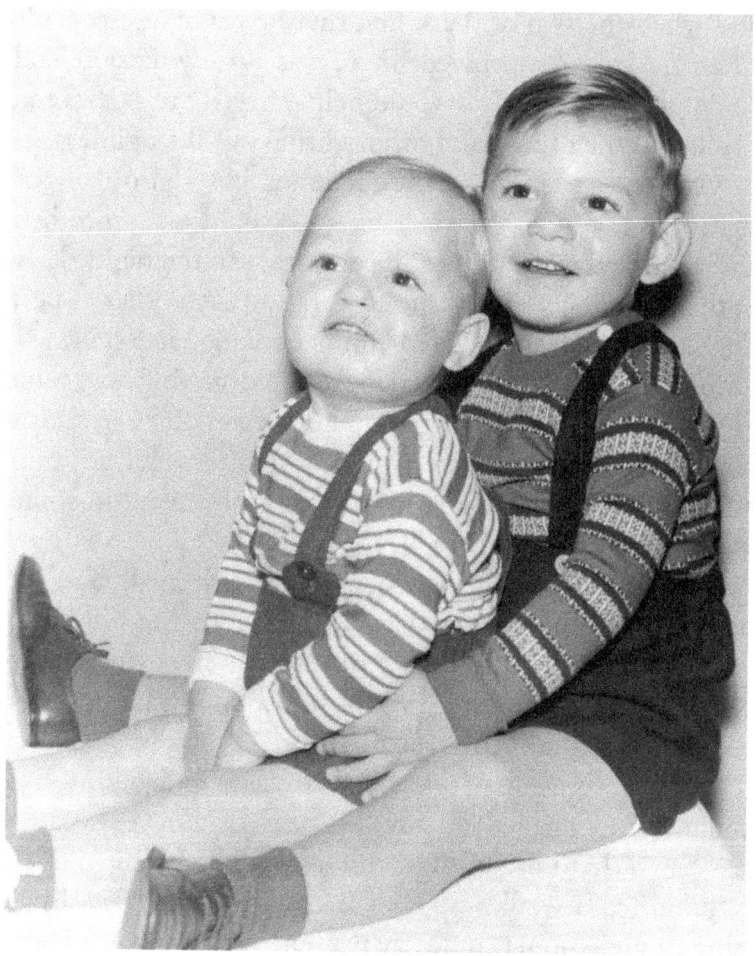

Jesse and Lee Taken in 1959
shortly after adoption

Chapter 2

DNA

Back at the computer, this ancestry site is really wanting me to give them my DNA. These little leaves are floating around flashing "DNA! DNA! DNA!" I click on other tabs. I look at Facebook and type in the name "Donna Hurst" again and again expecting to find different results. That is the name of the woman on my birth certificate.

I go to Google and type in the same thing and I see the same dead ends. Click Ancestry. Click Facebook. Click Google. Click Ralph Lauren Clearance Sales. I know that last one isn't going to help me find my birth family, but I do enjoy a good bargain and it's what I do when I'm bored. I know it's dumb. It's so dumb, in fact, that sometimes when the packages arrive I hide them from John so he doesn't give me shit for spending money. It's weird, I know.

My brother, Lee, isn't as obsessed about this stuff as I am. Lee and I were adopted together as brothers when I was two years old and he was ten months and a day younger than me. I mean, he's still that much younger than me, it's just my way of saying that Lee was about a year old and that we were born really close together.

My dad tells us we were a mess when they brought us home from *Boys and Girls Aid Society*. Back at that time there wasn't much help for adoptive parents. As my dad puts it, "Once your check cleared, you were on your own!"

My parents used to tell us that Lee was still on drugs when they brought us home, and that, clearly, I had been abused in some way. He thinks that because whenever I would walk around someone I would go way outside their legs, as if I was trying to get out of kicking distance.

We were pretty skinny, and I think that my parents thought that if they brought us home and fattened us up and gave us love, that everything would be all better. It's pretty clear things were more complicated than that, and I know my dad wishes he could have gotten his money back.

Our older sister was nine years old when they brought us home. She was their biological daughter. We were so radically different as kids that I think my parents were shocked that their parenting didn't automatically work on us the way it did on Sis.

I wonder if it would help Lee if I found our birth family. Lee has had a tough life. He's been in and out of prison for 22 years. He's been married too many times to remember, and he lives his life on the edge.

Lee's in a biker gang, which is pretty much his whole family now. He's married to Rosa again, which is great for everyone. She's a social worker and has had her own rough life, but I think she has been a stabilizing force for my brother. Whenever I talk to her about this Ancestry site she tries to be patient but then she'll just kind of snap and say, "God dammit, Jesse! Just do it already!"

It's not like this is the first time I tried to search for them. I was bugging them so much at the *Boys and Girls Aid Society* that I swore there was probably a picture hanging up in their office like a *Help Wanted* poster saying, "Do Not Talk To This Man!"

I understood the files were sealed back in 1959, and that if they did actually give me information, they could get in big trouble. I got it. I just found it frustrating.

They were able to provide my birth name, which was "Jesus Martinez," my biological parents' names, and their race. At one point I went to a Catholic Church to see if they had any information on me being baptized. I figured with a name like Martinez—not to mention Jesus—there was a strong chance I was Catholic. The priest met with me and told me that he wasn't able to release any baptismal records, but if I was concerned, I should go to a private space and accept Jesus Christ as my personal savior. I tried to avoid rolling my eyes. Clearly, he missed the point.

My brother's birth name was José Martinez. We both pass for white, but I sometimes wonder what his *White Power* biker gang would think about that fact.

I know this sounds unbelievable, but I have a memory of my parents telling me that we were going to call him Lee. I remember stomping my feet and saying "No! His name Zay! Not Lee! Zay!" Can you really remember things when you're that young? I know that sometimes people think they have memories from their youth that are really just stories they heard over and over when they were growing up. That doesn't seem like that would be the case though, because my parents didn't like to talk about changing our names. Plus, there is that detail about my not being able to pronounce José and shortening it to something a kid would say. It definitely feels like a memory to me.

My parents changed my name from Jesus to Jesse, which I guess is pretty close. But changing José to Lee is more extreme. I know "Lee" is a family name, but I also know that they weren't crazy about advertising the fact that their kids were Mexican. They weren't "White Power Biker Gang" level racists, but they were still really prejudiced, and this was the early 1960s. Adopting kids was enough of a secret without adding in another culture to the mix.

I wonder what my mom would think of me looking for my birth mother. I waited until my mom died to start checking out this website. I miss her so much. Alzheimer's is a horrible disease. My poor dad was really patient with her, especially when she kept making them move apartments in their retirement community. She would get all paranoid about her neighbors. He would try to keep her calm, but she would be so insistent it was just easier to move.

I remember trying to be patient with her. "You know Mom, I know you're scared, but I don't think the Johnson's are really listening to you. Do you remember how hard of hearing they are?"

She would calm down for a few minutes and then start in again, pulling me in to tell me in a low voice, "Did I tell you about the Johnsons? I know they think I don't know, but I do. I can tell they're listening to everything we are saying."

My dad would rub her back and say, "Now Trudy, honey, it's OK. They're not listening to us. We're not that interesting. Would you like Jesse to make you a snack?"

This would play out over and over and I would be exhausted just being there for a visit. My poor dad. My poor mom.

I understand paranoia. I just wish she didn't have to go through that level of fear. There at the end, she was in the Memory Care unit without him—in a completely different assisted living facility. I'm not even sure what she knew or didn't know.

My older sister died a year before my mom, and if there is a silver lining to my mom having Alzheimer's, it's that she didn't have to go through the pain of losing Sis. God, now I'm getting that lump in my throat again. Big breath. It's been some time since my last cigarette. This is why John keeps texting me to get off the computer. He knows it's deep for me.

Back to the back door with my arm out in the heat, I peek out my head to take a drag off my American Spirit.

When Lee and I found out we were adopted, one of the things we learned was that we were part Native American on our mom's side. My dad would actually bring home books on different tribes, and when we were traveling somewhere there was anything like a tipi on display or totem poles or something like that, he would take his time helping us learn about it. Of course, we had no idea about the differences in tribes, and we were using the word Indian, or Injun, because it was the 1960s and no one used the term Native American.

It's kind of nice to remember my dad doing that for us. I've been pretty angry at my dad lately. I know he's in a lot of pain from losing my sister and my mom so close together, but it doesn't excuse the way he treats me and Lee. I mean, he actually told both of us that we were out of his will at my mother's funeral. I'm serious. I remember Lee telling him to go fuck himself and I just looked at him like I couldn't believe what was happening, afraid of making a scene.

"Jesse, god dammit, why do you care what these assholes think? He's the one that should be embarrassed, not us. Fuck him. Fuck his money. Fuck all these motherfuckers." Holding in feelings isn't Lee's strength.

What's worse is that during my sister's funeral there was a time where they played music and showed pictures of my sister with different family members, and there weren't any pictures of me or Lee. Who does that?

My sister's husband, Dan, put together the photo collage, and I don't want to assume that he did that on purpose—I'm sure it just slipped his mind. I would expect more from my dad though, telling us that we were out of his will. Two funerals, back-to-back, where Lee and I felt even more shitty than we already did from losing our sister and our mom.

Immediately after my mom died, my dad told me that I could pick out one item from my mother's possessions. I took her diamond necklace and her diamond earrings. I know I was only supposed to take one thing, but I figured "her diamonds" counted as one. I gave one of the earrings to Lee and we both wore them to her funeral. Sometimes it feels like my dad forgets that Lee and I were in mourning too. Grief is a complicated beast, and sometimes anger spills out in places where it shouldn't.

Lee isn't talking to my dad at all right now, which is Lee's way. Lee went over to mom's apartment in the memory care unit after she died and my dad was there. He told Lee that the only thing he would give him that belonged to my mother was the leftover bar of soap that was in my mom's bathroom, and damned if Lee didn't take it.

I still talk to my dad on the phone, and I may have mentioned that I was looking at this Ancestry site and he may have told me "Good luck with that," but then he launched into telling me about something he had seen on *Fox News*, and to be honest, I just sort of tuned him out at that point.

I remember the day we found out we were adopted. I'm guessing we were in 2nd and 3rd grade. Lee came up to me after school and said, "Jesse! Timmy Stevens just told me that I didn't come out of Mom's tummy."

"Why did he say that?"

"I don't know, Jesse. That's why I'm asking you. I wanted him to share the ball with me and he told me to get lost and I told him to shut up and then he said that I didn't come out of my mom's tummy and then he turned around and walked off."

Neither one of us really understood why Timmy would say that, and given how feisty Lee could be, I was a little surprised he didn't react more strongly to Timmy, but waited to get more information. We asked our mom what

Timmy meant, and she was pretty shocked.

"Now boys, do you remember when I told you how babies are born? Well, in most cases, babies do grow inside their mother's tummy. That was the case with Sis."

Lee and I looked at each other and then looked at her and nodded.

"Well, with you boys, you grew up in a different mommy's tummy. Unfortunately, she wasn't able to take care of you. You two are so special that we went and actually chose you to come live in our house."

I asked, "Where did you choose us from? Was it like a store or something? Like a toy store?"

She looked at me and smiled.

"It wasn't a store, but it was a place that helps parents find very special babies that need a home. We felt very lucky to have chosen the two of you."

Lee asked, "So how come Timmy knows about us?"

My mom was friends with Timmy's mom and I am sure he overheard the two of them talking. My mom sighed.

"I don't know why Timmy knows, and I wish you would have heard it from us directly. I'm sorry he told you. It's nothing to be ashamed of, it just means that the two of you are really special and that we chose you to join our family."

I saw an opportunity. "Well, if we're so special, could we get a couple of cookies?"

My mom looked relieved, and Lee looked at me with a big smile. If I could use this angle to get some sugar, I was going to go for it. I knew there were cookies in the cookie jar and we didn't usually get a treat until after dinner. I'm sure my mom was just relieved to end the conversation, and probably wished she would have offered us cookies to put it off.

When we were a little older, my mom explained that after Sis was born, she and my dad found out they couldn't have any more babies the natural way, so they contacted an agency that helped connect them to children who needed homes. Over the years, we have heard different stories about my parents' fertility issues. My mom said that it was her issue, and my dad said that it was his issue, and in some ways I guess it's a sweet for each of them to protect the other one. None of us actually cared about their fertility issues, and we definitely would not have judged either of them.

I was a pretty curious kid, so I continued to ask my parents about my birth family. They told us that our mom was Native American and couldn't look after us. They also told us she was a prostitute, which is why we were so close in age. Now, I don't know why in the world you would share that with a kid, and again, I know sometimes our memories aren't always reliable. I do remember that though, mostly because I had never heard that word before. When I figured out what it meant, I mostly just pictured a woman wearing harem pants and looking a little bit like Jeanie on *I Dream of Jeannie* did, but Indian. So really, I kind of pictured my birth mom looking like Cher when she dressed up like an Indian. God, no wonder I turned out gay! I wonder what Lee pictured our birth family looking like. He doesn't really talk about it, but he does say that finding out we were adopted didn't make him feel special. It just made him feel different.

I don't know what I expect from this Ancestry site. I don't know what I really want. I don't know why I feel like I need to get answers to fill in the holes inside my soul. What if I find this woman and she's not Cher in a headdress, but someone who is so broken she had to give away her two babies? What if she doesn't want anything to do with us? I don't know how I would handle that kind of rejection.

On the other hand, what if meeting her will help me make sense of my life in a way I can't even imagine? What if I finally feel some connection that I haven't ever felt from my adoptive family besides Lee?

I walk outside to the ashtray, feet burning through my flip flops, and then go back to the computer. I open up Ancestry.com and I hit "Sign up," give them my information—even signing up for the DNA part—take a deep breath, and hit Send.

Sister Trudy, with her new brothers, Jesse and Lee

Chapter 3

House On Fire

My DNA kit arrived today! It's this white box and it contains a little instruction manual, a vial to collect my spit, and some chemicals to add to it. There is a self-addressed envelope, and it's even paid so I don't have to go to the post office to hand over my spit. I wonder how you answer the questions about liquid or perishables when it comes to the sample. It doesn't look like It takes much, actually, but it does say I need to abstain from eating, drinking, smoking, or chewing gum for 30 minutes. I think that seems manageable, although now that this is real, I could really use a cigarette.

John is trying to be supportive. When I talk to Lee about it, he just kinda says the minimum to agree and then moves to another topic. Mostly he moves on to complain about our dad, which would probably be what I would be talking about if I still lived in the same town. I don't know if he's just not interested in this process of looking for our birth parents, or if he's scared. Maybe he just wants me to do all the work and tell him how it turns out. That would be typical.

I remember once when Lee and I were kids and our parents were out of the house—I think it was on a Saturday. Sis was watching us, but that didn't mean we were in her eyesight or anything.

Sis was nine years older than us, so she got stuck babysitting us all the time. There was this big barrel of packing material in the basement and I'm not sure which one of us had the idea, but we started lighting matches and throwing them into the barrel. We didn't think anything would actually happen. I mean, how many times had we all stood around the campfire trying to get it to start. My dad would make this elaborate tipi and he would get down on his hands and knees and blow on it. At first he would always try to get us to help him, like he was teaching us or something, but then he would end up pushing us out of the way and doing it himself. He'd be swearing under his breath and my mom would pretend she wasn't hearing him, until she couldn't help but comment.

"Harlan, it's just a fire. Do you have to swear? The other campers will hear you"

"Dammit Trudy, what kind of wood did you get for this thing? This must be wet or something. I hope you weren't counting on s'mores tonight!"

It would always end up starting, and he would let out a big breath, and Lee and I would get ready with our long sticks to stir it while Sis and my mom would get out the marshmallows. I swear, it was a lot of effort to start a fire.

Well, the fire in the basement didn't take a lot of effort. It started pretty quickly. At first we just started to blow on it, and yes, we were swearing to each other, trying to deny that this was really happening. As the flames got higher though, the adrenaline set in and I looked around to try to figure out how to put it out.

"Lee! Go upstairs and tell Sis. Go get some water!"

Lee's eyes were huge and he bolted upstairs yelling for Sis. I just remember saying "shit shit shit shit shit" as I tried to find something in the basement to put on it to smother it. Sis came running down the stairs with Lee behind her carrying a glass of water. Bless his heart.

"What the hell is going on? Jesse! Go upstairs NOW. Go get the hose!"

Now remember, this was in the 60s and it wasn't like it is now with fire extinguishers in everyone's kitchen. I ran outside and was frantically unwrapping the hose while Sis took it and headed downstairs. Once the fire was out the whole house was filled with smoke. Lee and I were both crying at that point, and begging Sis not to tell on us. We opened windows, trying to get rid of the smell of smoke. We knew my parents would totally go ballistic. My dad had been buying these panels for the walls in the living room. He would buy two panels with each paycheck and here we had almost burned the entire house down. How many paychecks would that take?

Well, Sis didn't need to tell my parents because it was obvious when they got home there was a fire. I don't want to go into what my dad did when he was upset, but it wasn't pretty. I don't remember Sis getting into trouble for not being a better babysitter. Of course she wouldn't get in trouble. She never got into trouble, ever.

It seems like my mind automatically thinks of all the times when we were little monsters, getting in trouble and having conflict with my parents. It wasn't all like that though, and I need to remember some of the good times too.

When I was in 3rd or 4th grade, my dad built us a jungle gym in our backyard. He thought that it might help with our coordination and give us an outlet to burn off some energy. He ordered a kit that arrived in the mail and required assembly. It really was quite the play structure. There were three stories with landings in between them, and a fireman's pole to slide down. He made a big deal about staking it down into the ground, knowing that Lee and I would definitely test it to its limits. There was a canvas top to help provide some shade, but those steel poles still heated up in the summer sun. I can only imagine kids who grow up here in Palm Springs. You could seriously burn yourself on something like that in the summer.

I think about the work that it took my dad to build that thing. He could have just made us ride our bikes to the park. I try to remember these things when I'm feeling angry with him or misunderstood by him. I remember how he bought me a clarinet in the 5th grade because he knew that I wasn't athletic. I'm sure that was a little hard for him. I was so much taller than other kids my age, I am sure that part of him was hoping for a basketball star. Instead, he encouraged me to join the school band because he thought it would help me fit in with a group of kids and help me find something I loved. Yes, he was the one who would dole out the discipline, but there were good times too.

The Christmas that I was in 4th grade, Lee and I came downstairs to find two Schwinn bikes under the tree with a note that said they were "from Santa." We pretty much lost our minds. I remember each bike had a big banana seat and they had motorcycle handlebars.

"Look Jesse! Santa really is real. I told you so. I'm going to ride this thing all over everywhere."

I started to tell Lee that it didn't actually mean that Santa was real, but I stopped myself. I remember looking at Lee and then looking at my parents and everyone was smiling, even though my parents weren't getting the credit for buying us those bikes. For once I knew enough to let Lee win the argument and to enjoy the surprise.

Maybe that was the experience that planted the seed for Lee to develop a love of motorcycles later in life. My dad had to teach us how to ride them, and even though we didn't take long to figure it out, that was a process that required some patience. My mom was the one we would go to if we were upset or hurt, and of course there were a million things she did every day to show us love. I know a lot of dads don't do that much and some don't even stick around. My dad definitely stuck around.

It's been an hour now since I had a cigarette, so I take out my little vial and spit into it. You have to fill it to this line and then you add some liquid called "stabilizing fluid." You shake up the tube for five seconds and then put it in a little pouch and then in the box to mail it back to the company. Pretty simple, really. I have had at-home colon samples that were more complicated. Now I just need to wait for 6 to 8 weeks for them to tell me they can't help.

I know I should stop thinking like that, but I can't help but expect the worst. I could dream about the best possible results, but I'm not sure what that would even look like at this point in my life. I doubt I will get a letter in the mail, "Congratulations Jesse! Your mom really IS Cher! Look Chastity—or I guess it's Chas now—you have two brothers!" No offense to Cher, who was definitely not old enough to be my mother.

The hopeful part wants to find someone wonderful, but the more realistic part of me thinks about what Lee and I have gone through, and I wonder what would happen if we find our mom and she's a horrible person. I mean, what if she really was a drug addict prostitute? What are the chances she's even alive? It's back to walking that tightrope between hope and fear, optimism and protection, fantasy and reality.

While Lee hasn't acted that interested, Rosa has been a little more into it. She needs something to cheer her up right now. Rosa's daughter, Mellissa, was killed in a car accident a few months ago and Rosa's mostly been in bed trying to survive. My heart just breaks for her and for everyone who was close to her. Rosa and Lee were married years ago and then they split up and she married someone else and had three daughters.

I had not been close to Mellissa and Rosa's older daughter, Holly, as they weren't in the house when Lee and Rosa got back together. I'm close to her younger daughter, Tabitha, though. She's a hoot. I have lost people in my family that I have been close to, but it's nothing compared to losing a child, even if they are grown.

On top of the grief, Rosa has had some physical issues with rheumatoid arthritis, so in addition to the emotional pain, she's also in physical pain. Lee has been working more hours, because Rosa hasn't been back to work since this happened. Right now she's on medical leave. Lee has been away at work, and he's also been trying to take care of everything in the house, and has been really sweet with Rosa. I wish my dad would be sweet to Rosa, or at least acknowledge what they are going through as a family. For such a smart man, he can really be dumb sometimes.

Rosa has always called me her "Hollywood Husband," which is pretty funny. I actually did a little modeling when I was in my early twenties and living in LA. There's this one photo of me, with my silk shirt and tight pants, hand on my hip and my smoldering stare right into the camera. Sizzling hot, if I do say so myself. One might even say a young Erik Estrada. Those were the days. If only I had been discovered. With those looks and my dramatic personality, I could have totally ended up in pictures. Sometimes I will take out those photos and imagine what it would be like if I had actually made it big.

I think for Rosa, the nickname is more about how much more flashy and stylish I am compared to Lee. I mean, Lee is flashy in his own way. His body is covered in tattoos and he has long hair. He's usually wearing his motorcycle gear and he even wears more jewelry than I do most of the time. He's definitely not anyone that would be described as

"Hollywood," unless there was a movie being made about bikers.

I adore Rosa, and just wish I could ease her pain. I usually make her laugh, but that feels impossible right now. Hopefully this project will give her a little something to look forward to and to get excited about. I send her texts and sometimes she texts right back and sometimes it takes time. I understand. I have waited this long to get answers, and I just want her to come along for the ride at her own pace.

I don't tell Rosa this, but I have been praying for her. I don't think it would make her upset or anything, but I just know that sometimes you don't really want to hear about someone else's God when you feel like yours has let you down.

When we were growing up, my parents were really involved in the church. One year for Christmas when we were in 4th and 5th grade, we were given these religious books that had little stories in them that were supposed to teach us moral lessons. Every Wednesday night after dinner we would have Family Devotional Night, where Lee and I would take turns reading a story out loud and then discussing it as a family. Sis was there too, but clearly these were written for younger kids and clearly we were the ones who needed these lessons in morality.

I remember the story of the Good Samaritan. I read it out loud, and then we talked about how it applied to our lives. I remember feeling like I should be friendly to all the kids at school who didn't have any friends. I think I even thought about trying to have mercy on Lee when he was annoying me. Maybe reading that story somehow planted a seed that led me to be a case manager at Cascade Aids Project, and a caregiver now. I definitely had my share of Good Samaritans that helped me when I was struggling. I also had tons of people who walked on by, even when it was obvious I needed help. It's tough, trying to figure out how to be a helper without enabling someone. Those Bible stories we read don't get into the complications of addictions and boundaries and what does and doesn't help. I wonder if my biological mother had someone helping her when she decided to give up her two kids.

Sis and I used to talk about religion a lot as adults. She was a minister and had some pretty strong beliefs about all of it. Most of the time we could talk in a way that was respectful of the other person's opinion, especially when I brought up my feelings about Christians who use their beliefs to discriminate against gay people. I don't feel like there's this old guy with a beard lounging around on the clouds looking at all of us, but I do feel like there's something greater than myself. It helps me feel less alone. I want that for all of us, but I really want it for Rosa right now. I should text her and tell her about my spit sample. I might even say something like, "I know Lee doesn't give a spit." They will both roll their eyes, but it might make her smile, which is something she needs right now. We all do.

Chapter 4

Dance For Us, Jesse

It's been a week since I sent in my little sample of spit. I got an email from the Ancestry site saying that they received it and that it would take 6 to 8 weeks to process it. I wonder how it works. I know the basics of how DNA works, but it is still a little mind blowing how they can figure this stuff out. I half expect them to send me an email saying,

"Dear Mr. Scott, we were unable to read your spit due to all the medications in your system as well as the fact that it's soaked in nicotine."

Hopefully their little machine can do its work and see past all the other chemicals floating around inside my body. Those chemicals have been such a part of my routine for so many years that I didn't even think about it until I sent away that vial of spit. I'm so used to giving over vials of blood over the years that the spit just seemed cute.

I have been playing phone tag with this rich lady from L.A. who might hire me to be a caretaker for her son. He's in his 20s, and was in a swimming accident in the ocean and is now in a wheelchair. It sounds like an interesting gig. Apparently I would drive into L.A. and stay there for five days every other week in some extra bedroom or maid's quarters or something. I'm not sure how that would go with leaving John here by himself. Maybe that might make him appreciate me more, with the heart growing fonder and all as they say. I have been out of work for a month now and although we're not together when John is at work, I am sure he wouldn't mind getting a little more of a break from me, especially if all I do is obsess over these websites.

I miss Jim and Milan. That was my last job. I was Jim's caretaker and Milan was his wife. I mean, she's still his wife, although Jim is dead now, so I'm not totally sure how that works. Jim was a sweet older gentleman who had a stroke. I helped him with everything: bathing, dressing, taking his medications, taking him to his appointments. I also cleaned their house and went to the store and cooked for them. Milan was so upset when he died that she asked if I could stay on and do the cooking and cleaning for her, but we both knew that wasn't something that could be sustainable. We were both in pain from his passing and just wanted to somehow keep things the same.

I called Milan earlier today to see if she would be a reference for me, knowing that of course she will give me a good reference. We spent about an hour on the phone catching up, even though I haven't been gone that long.

Most caretakers don't have as much of a role in a family as I did with them. After Jim died, Milan sent me to Washington D.C. to help put some of his affairs in order. She was his second wife, and his kids weren't thrilled to be around her, even though it had been some time since Jim divorced their mom.

Jim was a veteran, with a Gold Star, so my trip to D.C. actually even impressed my own dad, who is also a veteran. It didn't impress him as much as it would if I had joined the military, but clearly that was never going to happen. I mean, it's not like they would have me. If my country doesn't want me to fight for it just because I'm gay, then that is their loss. Don't get me wrong, I think that everyone has a duty to serve their country in some way. I'm just not much of a fighter. Maybe I could have helped in a different way, like in the medical field or something. I still respect it, and I know that was a huge part of my dad's life, it just wasn't for me, and clearly the feeling between me and the military is mutual.

My parents didn't exactly handle the whole gay issue any better than the military. I know, I know, it was a different time. I see parents now taking their gay kids to Gay Pride parades and it makes me tear up a little bit. I'm not tearing up because I'm jealous, I just feel so proud of how far this country has come in recognizing that supporting your kids, no matter their sexual orientation or gender or whatever, is such a way to express love. That wasn't my experience at all. My first memory of my parents reacting to me being gay was actually really strange.

I must have been in 1st or 2nd grade when my dad caught me wearing my mom's skirt. I had been caught playing with dolls and stuff before but the look on my dad's face this time felt different. That night, my dad came into my room and handed me my sister's nightgown and told me to wear it when I came down for dinner. When I came downstairs, everyone was sitting at the table eating dinner. When I approached the table, my dad got up and led me over to the corner of the room.

He put on Chubby Checker.

"You're going to dance for us, Jesse. If you want to dress up so badly, well this is your chance to put on a show."

The notes of "The Twist" started to fill the room, and I just stood there. Lee's eyes were pretty big, which makes sense as it was a really confusing scene. My dad was smiling at me in this weird way that wasn't a happy smile and he kept saying, "Go on now. You know you want to dance."

And so I did. I loved that song. If I'm being honest, dancing in that nightgown wasn't awful. I mean, I was really confused and I knew my parents were upset with me, but the actual dancing part was alright. When the song ended my dad got up and restarted the record player so I ended up dancing to that same song again and again while the rest of the family ate their meatloaf. Lee kept trying to look at me, while he nervously laughed.

My mom said, "Lee! Turn your chair around and eat your dinner. Just ignore your brother."

My mom started asking him questions about his day and it was like I wasn't even in the room until the record ended and my dad walked over to change it. I can't remember if Sis was even there, but I know she didn't stick up for me or tell my parents they were being cruel. I don't even know if she would have thought that was cruel when I think about it.

I'm not sure what he though it would accomplished. Maybe he was thinking that it would be the same experience as parents who catch their kid smoking a cigarette and then force their kid to smoke a whole pack, making them sick. I knew at the time I was supposed to be humiliated, and that was definitely part of how I felt. I didn't know the word "degrading" then but I felt it. I knew my parents didn't approve of me and the shame felt like a knot in my stomach. It just seems so bizarre now as an adult looking back. Bizarre and clearly ineffective. If anything, it didn't stop me from being gay, it only stopped me from being open about it.

I am sure that in the context of their conservative Christian household in the 1960s, a gay kid wasn't what they were expecting when they took home two babies from the adoption agency. Don't get me wrong, they weren't Bible thumpers or anything. We were very focused on church though. We had church every Sunday and those family devotion readings every Wednesday night. Typical "Leave It To Beaver" nuclear family.

There is a photo of me and Lee in our Sunday best posing for the church directory. Mom liked to dress us in clothes that were matching but not identical. There we are in our little plaid suits, in slightly different colors, but showing up the same in the black and white photo. I look so much older, as usual, and I'm sure, that morning, mom must have wrangled us into those suits. They were costumes, really, meant to portray this typical loving situation. If only my mom's two sons were as well behaved as Wally and Beaver.

It's funny now to think that my dad describes me as Eddie Haskell. I guess he's the worst character from that show. My dad still thinks I'm a smooth talker, and in some ways I can't completely disagree with him. If only Eddie was gay and more attractive.

Not long after the whole Chubby Checker Dance Party Incident, there was a carnival happening in our neighborhood. All the kids were dressing up in costumes and there were boardwalk games set up. My mom picked out a clown costume for me to wear, and she helped me put it together. For some reason, my mom thought it would be funny to have me wear balloons under my top so I looked like a clown with a couple of big boobies. Lee thought it was funny, but she didn't have him wear boobies with his costume. To this day I don't know if that was my mom's way of making up for the humiliation I felt when I had to dance for everyone, or if it was her way of having me experience public humiliation by being teased by neighborhood kids. Maybe it was an extension of the pack-of-cigarette "lesson" for kids who get caught smoking.

Well, if that was her motivation, it backfired. None of the kids made fun of me at all. In fact, when I think about it, none of the kids at school really ever teased me about being feminine or being a sissy or anything. I feel like my sexual orientation was a much bigger deal for the adults in my life, and the kids could care less, at least at that age.

I did a lot of stuff when I was a kid that I consider really boyish, and I got in trouble for that stuff too. I used to like to take things apart. Get out a wrench and take out screws and see how everything fit back together. I did it to the oven, the furnace, and the washing machine. Sometimes I would do it to my bed frame in my room. That one was the easiest to hide. My parents found it odd, and obviously they didn't want their major appliances falling apart.

"Dammit, Trudy, he did it again. I told you to hide the tools from him."

I think it was just odd to them because my older sister didn't do it. I figured out that it was easier to tell them I would stop, but then I would wait for them to go to sleep and I would get out a flashlight and do it at nighttime. When they would wake up to find out I had taken something apart they would see it as not only odd, but now it was deceitful, and it made me a liar. I still think it was a thing little boys do, but it just added to all the things my parents thought I did that were troubling.

When I was a kid I wasn't the only one to get in trouble. Lee was definitely in trouble all the time, but because we were constant playmates, it seemed like I would get in trouble for stuff Lee did, even though I wasn't the one doing it.

My parents thought I was the brains behind the operation. For example, I believed it might work to jump off the roof of the garage with an umbrella to use as a device to help you float down, almost like flying. Well, is it my fault that Lee was the one who wanted to go first? Once I realized it wasn't going to work, and that Lee was actually in a lot of pain, screaming bloody murder as he held his ankle, of course I climbed down instead of repeating the same thing. I didn't force Lee to go first, he was just braver than me. John says maybe Lee just wasn't as smart, but of course he doesn't say it to Lee's face, now, unless it's clear we're all joking.

So here we were, a couple of kids who were always talking in class, and who were always getting in trouble for dumb stuff. Not only would I get my butt whacked by the principal, which you could do at the time, I would get my desk moved out into the hallway, which was supposed to be a punishment. I thought it was a great way to get out of doing the lessons. I could just sit out in the hall and cut up as much as I wanted, with my classmates sneaking peeks at me while they were supposed to be paying attention. Those poor teachers.

When I was in 3rd grade and Lee was in 2nd grade my parents took us to see Dr. Linden Smith, who was a big deal child specialist in Portland. Supposedly, he's a really renowned guy. I have to hand it to my parents for at least finding us someone who was a big deal.

The school had been pushing them to do it. Even though I understood everything academically, I was really bored, and so I ended up being a bit of the class clown. I remember all my report cards said that I was bright, but under my behaviors it said, "Needs improvement, needs improvement, needs improvement!" So they took us somewhere to improve. Lee was an even bigger class clown in his classes, but unfortunately, his grades for the academic part weren't as good as mine.

Dr. Smith diagnosed both me and Lee with Attention Deficit Hyperactivity Disorder and he put us on Ritalin. That was when we got really crazy.

Instead of helping us calm down, it actually just made us a little paranoid. At least that's the way I remember it for me. I was paranoid about getting in trouble and paranoid my parents didn't want me, and so to make sure that didn't happen, I tried to cover my tracks, which included a lot of lying.

That was a big deal for my parents, especially my dad. He couldn't stand it. Looking back, I think that Lee and I had some abandonment issues as well as some PTSD. Those things weren't known back then though. I would get bored and misbehave, and then cover it up. My dad would find out and yell or spank me—usually both. I would be worried they would give me back and would try to be good, but then the whole cycle would start again. It was kind of crazy, really. Isn't it odd that both Lee and I ended up using so much meth as adults? You would think we wouldn't want that feeling again, but like most destructive behaviors, I doubt it's conscious. Plus, besides the paranoia and psychosis, meth can actually make you feel amazing. No one really talks about that part of it.

The next doctor I saw was Dr. Bradley, and this time I was the only one going to see him. I'm not sure if that's because they thought that I was the problem or because they could only afford to pay for one kid. Dr. Bradley was the one who made me do "The Lying Box." It was a technique he used where he gave me a shoebox and told me that every time I lied, I should write it down on a little piece of paper and put it in the box. The agreement was that my parents were not going to look in the box, but that I would bring it in when I saw him and I would read each lie to him and we would talk about it. I guess it was supposed to help me understand the root causes of why I was lying and the consequences of my lies. I suppose that on the surface that sounds like it makes sense. I just found it to be boring and it felt like one more chore or homework assignment I was expected to do each day.

I also felt like it was one more thing that made me feel different, even from Lee. I'm still not sure if my parents peeked in it when I was at school, or if Dr. Bradley was telling my parents what I was lying about. I never wrote anything about my feelings about boys. It was supposed to be treating my manipulative behavior, so I just focused on the lies they were expecting to hear from me rather than sharing areas of my life I was confused about at the time. I'm sure he wasn't cheap and I have to hand it to my parents for seeking out help from experts. I just wish any of those

Scott Church Family Photo 1963 Harlan, Trudy jr. , Jesse, Trudy sr. , Lee

experts or teachers, or gosh anyone really, would have told me I was doing my best to survive. Instead, the message was that I needed fixing. Or that I was just crazy.

Speaking of crazy, I can hear John in the other room watching *Fox News*. Someone needs to give the people on that channel a big old Lying Box.

Chapter 5

Nehru Collar and Elephant Pants

I can't believe my gay boyfriend is a Republican. He says it's because he's had to be on his own for so long, and he thinks the Democrats just want a bunch of handouts. Sometimes I try to get into it with him, but then he digs in his heels and we both just end up frustrated and upset.

I need to take my evening dose of medications. John doesn't seem to mind that the State of California pays for my medications through Medicaid and that the government gives me Social Security Disability payments. Somehow he thinks that's OK and thinks the Republicans won't take it away. Usually, we can just agree to disagree but there is an election for President this year so things will probably end up getting more heated between us. I try to ignore him talking about "Killery Clinton," and I can't really believe that Americans are dumb enough to vote for Trump. I will try not to gloat when he loses. If I find my birth mother, maybe that can be another person on my side politically, because it sure isn't my dad. He watches a lot of *Fox News* too.

John's independence was one of the things that attracted me to him when we first met. John was working on the carnival circuit as a vendor. He says he was "the original *Sham Wow* guy" even though he was selling other stuff besides *Sham Wows*. Once we were really together, he talked me into joining him.

We traveled all over the West Coast and we sold everything from jewelry to beds. I don't know why someone would spend thousands of dollars on a bed at a County

Fair, but who am I to stop a fool and his money from part-ing? We can both be pretty charming with customers and we would end up making enough money to take several months off and travel for fun or just hang out relaxing.

My dad once told me I was "a con artist" because I tell women the jewelry looks good on them when they are buying from my tent. I don't think that's being a con. I think that's being a good salesman. I was also really good at matching jewelry that looked good on my customers, so they would be excited about buying it. I thought I was just helping them feel better. What can I say? Women trust a gay man to tell them what looks good. Sometimes I would lay that on pretty thick, although only when John wasn't around.

Unfortunately, John also believed we should be quiet about our relationship in those settings too, which seemed pretty silly to me, but I didn't care enough to put my foot down. The carnival circuit has a bit of a hierarchy. We ven-dors saw ourselves as superior to the people who controlled the rides. The folks selling food were a step above the ride operators, and the vendors were at the top.

I didn't get a heavy homophobic vibe, but there also weren't a lot of people who were openly gay or openly a gay couple. It was John's process so I decided to support him.

While we would see some of the same folks on the cir-cuit, we weren't that close to any of them anyway, and John and I can both pretty easily pass as straight. We are a bit of a "Bert and Ernie" couple, as I'm tall and dark (and hand-some!) and John is almost a foot shorter than I am and bald. I think his bald head is sexy, which is another thing I didn't say to the people we met in the circuit.

It was a pretty interesting experience, working in that environment, but I never want to go to a fair again, espe-cially now that I know how much that stuff is marked up.

Eventually, the travel started to wear on us and I was having some health issues that needed some attention. We decided to get the jobs we have now, and spread out the work like normal people. I don't miss the travel we did for work, but I miss the time we had off together, especially when Les wasn't hanging around.

When I think about my childhood I try to remember some of the good times we had too. Every year we would go to the beach and camp for a week or two. Lee and I loved to run around on the wide stretch of sand, with the waves of the Oregon Coast crashing behind us. Sis would go for walks or read. I wonder what it was like for her on those trips. I wonder if we drove her nuts, too.

Sis was so much older and such a good girl. Lee and I had each other and when we were home she could be off with her friends. During our vacations, she was on her own. Maybe she got lonely. I wish I could call her up and ask her now that I'm thinking about it. Sis has been gone for three years now, and I keep forgetting that I can't just pick up the phone. How unfair that my parents had two sons with so many struggles, and a perfect daughter that turned out to be a minister, and she is the one they lose. It's not fair.

I remember going to Rooster Rock with my mom, Lee, Sis and her friend, Helen. Rooster Rock is in an area in the Columbia River Gorge, which is just outside of Portland. It's a spectacular area with lots of waterfalls and really lush forest. It feels like you are somewhere special, even though it's less than an hour's drive from Portland. The river is so big that you can barely see any details on the shore on the other side, and the current is fast and strong. We knew that it was different from going to the pool, but not as intense as going to the coast.

My mom was one of the only ladies at the time to wear a bikini. My mom had a lovely figure and my dad was fully in support of her showing it off. She would shave her eyebrows and paint on new ones that looked a lot like Lucille Ball's in "I Love Lucy." She would put on her fake eyelashes and her lipstick, and would keep her hair bleached blonde and in a short little perm. While Lee and I would play in the sand, my mom would be working on her tan with her cat eye sunglasses on, and Sis would need to make sure we didn't go too far into the water.

I'm not sure what Lee was doing, but I remember Sis and her friend playing with a beach ball. When the ball flew out of their hands and rolled into the river, I ran out into the water to grab it. Rooster Rock is a point in the Columbia River Gorge that has a long sandy beach, but the sand is cut out by the rush of the strong river and it forms a bit of a shelf below the surface. All of the sudden I was pulled into the water, and I distinctly remember not having anything to place my feet onto. I was terrified, and couldn't get my head above water. I have no idea if I was screaming or floundering or just silenting floating away. Suddenly I was pulled out of the water and dragged up on the shore by my mother, who was yelling at me.

"Go lie down! Go lie down!"

She kept yelling at me to go lie down on the beach blanket. The whole thing happened so fast and the fear I had when I was under water was intensified when I saw my mom panting and shaking and trying to calm herself down. I guess we both needed to go lie down. I had not seen her look scared before, and even though I didn't understand the gravity of the situation, I knew enough to know that I had caused my mom to freak out. She kept telling me to lie down, and so I did until we both got our breathing back under control.

When we were in grade school and Sis was in high school, my parents invited a foreign exchange student to come live in our home. It was somehow arranged by our church.

The student, Motoko, was a young woman from Hiroshima, Japan. Her parents ran an orphanage there, and took in babies that had been impacted by the war. She was 18 or 19 years old, and must have been studying at Portland State, although I admit my memory is a little hazy about the details. We were all so excited for her to arrive, but were not prepared for her reaction when she came into our living room and saw my dad's war medals hanging up in a case on the wall. My dad had been proud of his experience in the military, but clearly didn't think through the impact that his medals would have on this poor young woman who happened to be from the same people he had been shooting at in the war. My parents apologized and put away his medals for the next couple of years when she stayed in our home.

I think it was great for Sis to have someone else in the house who was closer to her own age. In a lot of ways she really did her best to try to relate to us, but it just felt like we had a third parent most of the time. Sis was a pretty serious girl. She always had her nose in a book or was knitting something or sewing something. She wasn't the most popular girl in school, but she wasn't picked on or anything either. She looked a bit like my mom, but wasn't quite as glamorous as my mom. You would never catch her painting on eyebrows or wearing false eyelashes.

One time my parents bought her a "fall" that was the same shade as her hair so she could look like she had more hair. I think they still have those now, but I don't know if they call it a fall anymore. It's like a small part of a wig that you clip into your hair to make it look longer or more full.

Sis was so excited, and would put it up in a bun or ponytail or whatever other updo she could come up with at the time. I know my mom helped her figure it out and my dad just nodded and would sometimes sneak an eyeroll at us boys. Lee would giggle and I didn't have the heart to let my dad know that I would rather be talking to my mom and sister about glamor.

Sis had the same name as my mom, and her friends called her Trudy. Lee and I called her Sis, and my dad called her Tuna. As if I needed more proof that my dad doesn't have a gay bone in his body. She didn't seem to mind, and if she did she didn't bring it up or ask him to stop.

Sis sewed her own clothes and even made her own prom dress. One time she made me a really cool shirt with a Nehru collar and elephant pants with huge flared bell bottoms, which were perfect for the times. I loved that outfit, and it really meant a lot to me that Sis did something to be nice to me, not out of any sense of obligation, but because she thought I would like it.

My mom let me wear the shirt, but told me that I couldn't wear the pants because they were too feminine. I had worn them to school once and no one had said anything. So again, this felt like something that was being turned into something that was more about my parents own hang ups, than what the kids my own age thought.

When Sis graduated from high school she went to Portland State University her first year and then she applied to study in Stuttgart, Germany. I know that she was inspired by having Motoko in our home, but part of me wonders if she wanted to go have her own adventure where she could get away from our family and find out who she was on her own.

Sis left when I was 10 years old. She flew out of Vancouver, British Columbia, so my parents ended up making a whole vacation out of it. We drove up to Seattle, and took a ferry to Victoria, Canada. We went to the Butchart Gardens, and walked around downtown and in different parks where there were totem poles. We took another ferry to go to Vancouver and explored there too. I just kept thinking about what a huge journey it was just get her on the airplane, and my brain couldn't imagine how long it would take her to fly to Germany. I remember my mom getting tearful and my dad asking her a million times if she had everything. I wish I could say that Lee and I were upset to see her leave, but to be honest, I think we just saw it as an exciting opportunity for her and a chance for us to have one less parent in the house. We had no idea that we wouldn't actually get to see her for the next few years and that our communication would be based on postcards, letters, and a very occasional phone call on holidays that was kept to five minutes so that it wouldn't cost us a fortune.

My brain is trying to avoid the next part of my childhood, because it's the part that starts everything going downhill. I would love to fast forward to just being here now, but I know I can't erase the stuff that was so hard. The next part is the part where my cousin Carol came to live with us and basically ended up ruining my life.

I need to go have a cigarette and think about something else for a while. If I lived in a normal place, I could go for a walk, but this desert heat won't allow it. Maybe I will go for a drive and tell Siri to blast some music and I can kind of dance around in my own little world without John rolling his eyes at me or telling me to keep it down. Luckily, I can still smoke in my car.

Chapter 6

A Little Like Pee

My cousin, Carol, came to live with us when I was thirteen years old. Carol was older than us, but not living on her own yet. I'm guessing she was 19 or 20 years old, which was almost as old as Sis. My aunt and uncle had been having some issues with her behaviors, although I'm not exactly sure what that meant. Sis was in school in Germany, and my parents had an empty room since Motoko had moved back to Japan. Maybe my aunt and uncle thought that their daughter would turn out like our perfect sister if she spent some time in her house. Maybe they didn't realize how much Lee and I were struggling. Or maybe they were just desperate and needing some time away. I don't know. My parents told them it was OK and so one day Carol and her golden retriever, Angel, showed up at our home.

Lee was pretty thrilled about the dog, and to be honest, I was pretty thrilled to have a girl in the house again. I missed Sis, even though she was so much older than us, and sometimes felt like another parent rather than a sibling.

Lee was still my best friend, but we were starting to have different interests. I would go to his baseball games and endure all the other parents asking why I didn't play. I didn't have a great answer, and I guess I still don't.

I'm just not into sports. I joke around now that I should be, if you think about it. It has everything I love: fit men, drama, and delicious snacks. John is really into sports and I will watch the Portland Trail Blazers, but otherwise, it's just not my thing. Back then, I was gravitating towards girls in general. They just seemed less threatening and a lot more interesting. I knew on some level that I should avoid these situations that were really masculine pressure cookers. Obviously that is more insightful than my young preteen self could articulate to the parents at Lee's games.

At first, with Carol, it was OK. She had some kind of medical condition involving her kidneys, so she had to take medications and we were told we couldn't rough house with her like we did with each other. Carol was pale and a little pudgy, and it became obvious that she didn't have a bunch of friends at home. I wasn't sure what these horrible behaviors were that got her sent to our house, but she wasn't that bad. At least at first.

Once Carol got settled in, we started noticing stuff. When she would get in trouble for something, she would burst into tears, which seemed strange for someone her age. Lee and I would talk back or lie to try to get out of trouble, but Carol would just start the water works and my parents would immediately back off. At first I was pretty concerned about her, but I started to notice how quickly the tears could be turned on and off and I realized it was just a big fake show. I also realized how she would immediately blame me for things that were her fault. My parents already thought I was a liar, so when I would deny it, I would end up getting in more trouble. I realized that Carol wasn't going to be my new girlfriend in the house, and we quickly started trying to set each other up.

I started by doing something stupid. I put a crushed up bag of chips in the washing machine while most of her clothes were in there. Unfortunately, instead of blaming Carol, my mom just assumed it was Lee. I felt kind of bad seeing Lee get in trouble, but if I came forward and admitted it was me, and admitted I was just trying to set Carol up, that wouldn't go over well at all. I just tried to console

Lee in our room and convince him that Carol had done it.

Carol started by taking my medications and hiding them up in the attic in a bunch of insulation. My parents were up there doing some kind of project, and while they were taking a break, Carol stashed the bottle in a place where they would find it. My dad went ballistic.

"God Dammit Jesse! I'm not spending an arm and a leg just so you can decide you aren't taking these pills!"

My parents were yelling at me, and telling me how long I was grounded, and I looked over to see Carol smiling behind her magazine.

That was the beginning, and looking back, it was the most straightforward of her setups. There was the time when my mom's wedding ring went missing near the sink. My mom had taken it off to do the dishes and assumed it had gone down the drain. My dad spent all day taking apart the drain, muttering to himself under his breath. My mom was pacing around, wringing her hands. I don't know why my dad didn't ask me to help. I could have easily taken a wrench to that pipe. The ring didn't show up, and my mom was crying all night, apologizing over and over to my dad.

Well, damned if that ring didn't show up a week later, in my mom's drawer, tucked into a sweater pocket. Again, my parents just lost it. When I asked why they thought it was me, my dad said that it was "too sophisticated" for Lee, and even though I had always assumed it was a good thing to be mature and sophisticated, this time they didn't agree. If they thought it was Carol, they never admitted it to us. Maybe they questioned her and she started crying or something.

The most creepy thing she did was to throw this little German nutcracker statue my sister had sent from Europe into the fireplace. My parents came home to find this and were totally bewildered. To make it even more weird, there was a vase of carnations on the table and she had used scissors to cut the heads off of 3 of them, leaving them on the table. Totally bizarre.

My parents sat us all down and had this little trial. We all denied everything, but Carol, through the tears, presented her reasons why this had to be me. She made it sound like I was angry at Sis or jealous or something, which was ridiculous. I missed Sis but I wasn't angry at her. I thought that little nutcracker made our house feel slightly more European. I mean, obviously I wouldn't be caught dead with carnations in my house now, but that's just because I have some taste.

I swear, thinking about Carol just gets me heated, even when I'm trying to make jokes about it. I know forgiveness is a virtue, and I don't like to live with all this anger. I try to think about what was going on for her at the time and why she felt the need to be so horrible to us. Well, to be fair, she wasn't horrible to Lee. I'm not sure why she picked me as her target.

I need a smoke. And something cold to drink. And a different childhood. At least the first two things are within my reach.

As I reach for some iced tea, I stop to look at our fridge. It's covered in magnets from all the places we have visited. There is a set of hula girls from Hawaii. The Canadian flag. The Rasta guy from St. Croix. Our friends started giving us magnets when they would travel, too, and now the whole thing is covered.

Like most of the things that are part of our house, I don't really notice them anymore. The magnets started as a way to remember our travels, but with all of these gifts from friends, it's also a reminder of places we have yet to see. There are also some erotic magnets that John found thrown in just to keep it interesting. I wonder what Carol's fridge looks like now. I'll bet Carol has a lonely life and never leaves her house to travel anywhere. I wonder if she still uses her tears to get out of things, and whether or not she has actually been diagnosed as a sociopath. Clearly, I am a long way from forgiveness.

The cigarette helps, but it doesn't keep the next part away. Part of me wants to stop and distract myself and think about something else. I can't though, and part of me wonders if I should even try. Looking for my mom isn't about hiding from my past. It's about diving into it and trying to have it make sense.

I am trying to figure out how much to blame my parents, or blame Carol, or blame myself. I have spent most of my life hating myself. Maybe if I look back with these older eyes, I can see what a setup it was having someone else come into our home. It seems so obvious to me now, but to this day, my parents haven't ever apologized for their decision to let Carol live with us. They still think I did those weird things, and that I'm still lying about it.

It was mid-October, 1970, and I was outside raking leaves when Carol came out with her dog. I tried to ignore her, but she kept messing with me.

"Why are you such a homo, Jesse? Lee says you never had a girlfriend or anything."

I told her to shut up, and I pointed out that she didn't have a bunch of guys knocking down our door. She was throwing the stick for Angel, and he kept getting closer and closer to the huge pile of leaves I had just raked.

"Well, that's just because I'm new here. I had a bunch of boyfriends at home.

I rolled my eyes.

"Can you please stop your dog from getting close to the leaves? I've been out here for like an hour already."

Carol looked me in the eye, and then she threw the stick directly into the pile, with Angel bounding through the leaves, scattering them all over the yard.

I admit I lost it. I started screaming at her and telling her I hated her and that I wished she would go back to her own fucking house. Carol was yelling at me too. The dog was jumping up and down and I'm not sure what happened, but in all the chaos Angel must have accidentally hit Carol's face with his paw, or something, because her lip started bleeding. Carol touched her hand to her lip and it was covered in blood. She looked me in the eye, and then she started screaming bloody murder and doubled over. My parents flew out of the house and into the backyard.

"Help! Aunt Trudy! Jesse just hit me! He hit me in the face and in the kidneys!"

My mom immediately ran to Carol to comfort her, and my dad turned to me with this look in his eyes like he was going to kill me. I kept yelling that she was lying, that I didn't touch her, but I was so upset I don't think I was making any sense. I dropped the rake and ran into my room and tried to move my desk in front of the door. My dad was pounding on the door, screaming at me to let him in, and I just sat on my bed hugging my knees, rocking back and forth.

I just realized I'm kind of rocking a little bit, back and forth, breathing heavy right now as I think about it. That was over forty years ago, but in some ways it feels like I'm right there in it. I remember staying in my room all night, trying to hear what my parents were talking about, with my mind spinning. They knew I was disruptive in class, even though I was smart and a pretty good student. They knew I was a liar. Now they thought I was violent.

By the time I finally came out of my room and talked to my parents, they were surprisingly calm. They told me I was grounded and they made me apologize to Carol, but they weren't as upset as I had imagined. I still remember the relief, as if a weight had been removed from my shoulders. The heaviness in my chest started to lighten and my stomach stopped hurting. I didn't go and hug them or anything, I knew better than to push it. I just remember feeling like everything was going to be alright.

Two weeks later, my parents told me that they were taking me to see another doctor. Lee and Carol left for school and we piled into the station wagon. It was a little strange that they were both in the car—usually my mom was the only one to take me to appointments. Maybe this was just another important fancy doctor and they wanted to get their money's worth or something. They let me pick the radio station, which was also unusual, but I wasn't going to complain. We were in the car for quite awhile, and even drove on the highway. I worried that my dad would blame me for "wasting all this damn gas," but he didn't mention it.

We pulled off the main road and drove onto this really long driveway, where a bunch of buildings were standing together. It looked a little like a college campus. The sign above the main entrance said "Dammasch State Hospital." I remember thinking I would tell Lee that Mom and Dad really did take me to the "Damn Hospital." He would think that was funny. My parents told them we were there to see a doctor and I eventually went into this guy's fancy office by myself. His name was Dr. Stewart.

I let Dr. Stewart know everything that had been going on with Carol. I explained everything very clearly and he sat there nodding his slightly balding head. He seemed to really understand my situation. He also asked me about my feelings towards boys, which was a little surprising that he would know that about me. I didn't really deny anything, but I didn't go into any detail either. After we talked for a while, he asked my parents to go in and see him and I waited in the waiting room and chatted with the receptionist and she gave me some candy out of a big bowl. Overall, this seemed to be going well.

Dr. Stewart called me back inside and he told me that he wanted me to go with a nurse while he talked to my parents some more. That was fine with me. I was used to going off to get my blood pressure and weight taken, and this just seemed like it was a little farther away than usual. It also smelled different from other doctor's offices I had been to in the past. The nurse wasn't into chatting, and she led me into this big room full of other people. She turned around and left, locking the door behind her. I wasn't sure what was going on. The smell was much stronger, and I didn't want to be rude about it, but I thought it smelled a little like pee.

That room was filled with a bunch of people, and they looked really strange. There was a small office that looked like a cage in the corner, and that seemed to be where the staff worked.

"Hey, I hate to bother you, but Dr. Stewart just sent me here and I think I need to get my blood pressure checked or something?"

"Hi Jesse. We have a bed for you where you can relax."

"No, I think I just need to get weighed and get my blood pressure checked. My parents are waiting for me with Dr. Stewart."

The staff looked at each other and one of them came out and led me over to a bed. It wasn't even a bedroom or anything, just a little cubby area with a bed in it.

"Here you go, Jesse. Why don't you try to get comfortable? You're going to be with us for a while."

"No, you don't understand. This is a mistake. My parents are waiting for me. I need to go back to them now."

The staff member ignored me at this point and walked back over to the rest of the staff. I followed him and the staff ignored me, turning around to talk to each other. I went back to the door and I started to pound on it, trying to get the nurse to come back and let me out. The other people there were looking at me and I realized this wasn't a normal doctor's office. This was a hospital.

I started yelling and banging on the door and the walls and at one point a couple of big guys came out of the staff office and grabbed me. I was screaming about wanting to see my parents, and the more I thrashed around and kicked and screamed, the more serious they looked at each other as if saying, "See, he really is violent, just like they said." My screams turned to sobs, and after a while I just sat in the corner, back in that ball, and cried, rocking back and forth, and I realized I looked just like everyone else.

The day I went to the state hospital was November 2nd, 1970. I will never forget that date. It was weeks before I saw my parents again, and almost a year before I saw Lee. Dammasch would be my home for the next 12 months.

Carol eventually moved out of our house, but left the dog. I don't think she ever admitted to anything, and to this day my dad still believes I was responsible for the lost ring, the burned nutcracker, the stashed meds, the bloody lip. I don't know if he regrets sending me away. If he does, he hasn't ever told me.

The first night I spent in Dammasch, I cried myself to sleep. My bed was in a pod that was the size of a large living room. There were five other beds in it, and instead of doors like a regular bedroom, there were wooden cabinets that were about five feet high that separated us from each other, and from the hallway. My bed was by the window on the far wall.

My first morning in Dammasch, I woke up at 6:30 a.m. to the sound of the sloshing of mop water. Someone was mopping the hallway, using one of those old metal pails and rag mops. I could hear the squeak of the pail and the movement of the wet mop on the floor, along with the faint smell of ammonia. This sound would later become a soundtrack to my mornings.

The other people in my pod were of various ages and states of mental illness. They separated us by gender, so we were all males, but not by age. Some people were shaking and/or drooling, and others looked like people I would normally see out in the world. It was really confusing, and I was bewildered about being there with all of them.

Our wakeup time was 6:30 a.m. every morning, and I was told to get dressed and ready for breakfast. We all changed behind our little dressers, which felt uncomfortable, having to immediately see everyone changing their clothes. Luckily, I had slept in my underwear, so I quickly threw on my clothes from the day before, and went over to the area where breakfast was served. A line of women came in, which I found out were the people living on "A Ward." Our ward was "F Ward." They joined us for meals, but were not allowed to go into the bathroom, the TV room, or the pods.

There was a buffet set up that included scrambled powdered eggs, bacon, powdered milk, and some potatoes that were like hash browns. It was pretty gross. I didn't even know things like milk and eggs could be powdered. I remember eating the potatoes and drinking water, which was all that my knotted stomach could handle that first morning.

I kept looking at all the other people, trying to understand how I fit into this scene. There was one woman, Anne, who was wearing a football helmet because she kept hitting her head with her fist. Anne was probably 18 or 19 years old. She would come to each person and ask "Do you love me? Do you love me?" over and over. If you didn't answer, she would stand there asking repeatedly until you did. So here I am on my first morning telling her I loved her just to make her go away. She eventually went over to the wall and banged her head on it until an aid came and took her away. I found it all to be very peculiar.

An aid came and tapped my shoulder and asked me to come to the "Aid Office." It was the cage looking office from the day before. The Aid Office was where all the nurses and aids worked, and it was surrounded in glass so they could see everyone. There was a sliding window that opened to distribute medications. The aids handed me a suitcase full of my clothes, which my mom had packed for me from home. I'm guessing it was in the trunk of the car where I couldn't see it. My eyes teared up seeing my stuff, probably because it confirmed that this wasn't some elaborate mistake. This was something my parents were in on, and they had even gone to the trouble of packing and hiding a suitcase full of my stuff.

I was assigned a chore, which was to go and mop the big bathroom. They told me I didn't need to mop the showers, but that I needed to get this done before I went to school. So I took my own metal pail and rag mop and headed into the bathroom to mop up pee stains. I didn't think to object. I did it, and they inspected it, and then I was escorted to the school.

The school had two doors; one for elementary age students, and one for high school. I was in 8th grade, so I went to the first door as they didn't have an option for middle school. I felt relieved seeing all the kids waiting in the hall. All the kids from the different units attended school, and for the most part, most of them looked more normal than the other people I had seen. I still don't know why they didn't have units for kids and units for adults. The kids were together in school, and for group therapy, but when we went "home" to our units at the end of the day, we were forced to interact with older people who had a whole bunch of problems that seemed much more intense than ours.

We were sleeping next to people who were pedophiles and criminals, and those were some of the people who looked normal. Some of the other people were in wheelchairs and would be shaking so much it was hard to look at them. It was almost like they thought the kids needed to see what their future held if they didn't shape up.

I know it's different these days.

That heaviness in my chest is back, but now my stomach hurts too. John is cooking some beautiful pork chops, and the whole house smells amazing. It's a long way from powdered eggs, that's for sure. I hope I can eat it, because he really did go to a lot of trouble. I know it's how he nurtures me. If I explain why I'm upset, he will tell me this is why I shouldn't be thinking about this stuff. He'll say, "The past is the past, you can't do anything to change it."

I know he's right. I'm not trying to change it, I'm just trying to understand it. I'm trying to realize that I was a mixed up thirteen year old kid who had a fight with a cousin, and who was gay, and those shouldn't be reasons to lock me up. I know that wouldn't happen now, and if it's not OK now, it wasn't OK back then. Big breath in. Big breath out.

Chapter 7

Stranger Danger

I opened up the computer this morning and checked my email to find an announcement from Ancestry. That pot of coffee I am brewing may be unnecessary, because I have so much adrenaline running through me right now, I feel like my head might explode if I add caffeine to the mix.

They make it really exciting too. There was an email with the heading "It's The Moment You've Been Waiting For..." and a button to push that stated "Explore Your DNA Results." When you get to the site it says, "Hello, Jesse."

John is already at work, and even though I sent him a text right when I saw it, he hasn't replied yet. He's been keeping his phone in his locker, and it's driving me crazy. Doesn't he know this is an Emotional Emergency? I texted Lee, too, and he hasn't written back yet, either. What's wrong with these people? Don't they understand how exciting this is?

The first part I look at is the Ethnicity Estimate for my DNA story. It's pretty cool. They actually show you a map and everything. It looks like I have 60% England and Northern Europe, 14% Scotland, 10% Ireland, 5% Norway, 4% Wales, and 7% Native American. Wow. That's a lot of white places for someone with a dad with the last name of Martinez. If they didn't include the Native American part, I might even think they had the wrong spit. Is it possible my mom gave them the wrong name or something when I was born? Was there a different dad? I have a lot of questions.

The next section is "DNA Matches." There are five

names that say they may be cousins. Like, actual real live cousins by blood. I hope these are better cousins than Carol. Clearly, they can't be any worse.

I keep looking for the names Hurst and Martinez, the ones that showed up on my birth certificate. There is someone named Marty Dick who is related to a Daisy Hurst. That looks promising. There's a Lorraine Hurst. This is so exciting! My heart is beating so fast that I need to get up and walk around the house a little bit to burn off some of this energy. Dammit, John, why aren't you here to share this with me?

As if on cue, my phone buzzes.

"Hey, what's the emergency? Do I need to come home?"

I may have left out what I was freaking out about. I may have sent the text "OMG I'm Freaking Out! This is an EMERGENCY." No wonder why he calls me a drama queen.

"No, you don't need to come home. I just got my DNA results from Ancestry and I'm really excited!"

"OK. Have fun. I need to go back to work. Do you want me to bring home some lobster or some steaks to celebrate?"

I roll my eyes at his lack of enthusiasm but know that he will make me a really nice meal, and that's just John's way of showing love and it's not something to complain about. Sometimes I pat my little pot belly and tell him it's all his fault. He pats his own, and says that at least we're fat and happy together.

OK, back to this Ancestry site. I write out these names, and start googling and looking them up on Facebook. This should keep me busy for a while. Thank God I don't have a job right now. I'm supposed to start working for the kid in Laguna Beach in a couple of weeks. I can't imagine seeing this while at work and not getting the chance to fully freak out.

This Marty Dick looks promising, and I'm not even going to make a joke about the last name. I mean, I love dicks. Sorry, I couldn't help myself. First I need to go smoke a cigarette. Then maybe I will be calmed down enough to drink some coffee and maybe my head won't explode after all.

My phone buzzes with text a message from Lee: "Jesus, Jess, what the fuck is your deal?"

I may have sent him a text saying "Lee! I'm freaking out! I'm finding out about our bio family now and you need to call me RIGHT NOW!"

I text Lee back, "I got the results back from Ancestry and I'm excited!"

He doesn't text back by the time I come inside from smoking.

I text him, "Lee! This is a big deal!"

"OK Jesse. Settle the fuck down. I just woke up."

Clearly, I'm going to have to celebrate on my own. Although, it still feels a little early to celebrate. I mean, these are just cousins. I'm not seeing my parents listed yet. Maybe I should pace myself with excitable texts. I don't want to be the little boy who cried wolf. I have to be careful about getting my hopes up. It's been something I have had to deal with my whole life. Well, maybe not my whole life. It is one more thing that I can relate back to my time at Dammasch. Just thinking about it takes me right back there as if it's all going on right now.

I remember I was trying to concentrate on the algebra problems I was working on when I heard the timer go off. I looked up at Dr. Mays, who looked at me and gave me a smile. She picked up a poker chip from a pile on her desk and dropped it into a clear glass bottle. The clink of the plastic chip on glass produced a nice little warm feeling in my head. I knew that if I could keep working on those problems I would hear it again in another fifteen minutes.

Dr. Mays was older than some of the other teachers at Dammasch, and she was definitely the most strict. She's the one who figured out this whole poker chip system. At first it was awful. Every 15 minutes after I did a good job behaving, a chip would fall into the jar. At the end of the day, Dr. Mays would write down how many chips I had earned, and she would give that number to the staff on the ward. When I wanted to buy something from the commissary, I had to use money AND chips.

I was furious when it started. Out of all fifteen kids in my unit, I was the only one doing the poker chips. It wasn't fair. Plus, I was the only 8th grader there working on GED books. Everyone else that did the GED books was older, already in high school. At least the GED books weren't as boring as the 8th grade work. It was impossible to get poker chips when I was so bored. I hated to admit that the clink felt good in my brain, but it did.

I also kind of liked that Dr. Mays was a doctor but she didn't prescribe medicine. She was "A Doctor of Education," which I didn't even realize was a thing. Now that I was off the Ritalin and the Dexedrine, I actually felt better. My dad seemed kind of disappointed when he heard that, as if it was proof that the fancy doctor I had gone to in Portland didn't know what he was doing.

I took medication for seizures, even though I didn't ever remember having a seizure, but when they measured my brain waves, they said it looked like epilepsy. I didn't mind the Dilantin. At least it didn't feel like my heart was beating too fast for my chest. Maybe Lee would feel better at home if he stopped taking that medicine, but every time I brought it up with my parents my dad said, "Don't you worry about your brother, he's just fine."

I didn't know if Lee was fine. I hadn't been able to talk to him or see him since I arrived at Dammasch. One time my dad visited and told me Lee had been getting in trouble and that it must be my fault, even though I wasn't there. God, Lee would hate the poker chips. He'd tell Dr. Mays to shove those chips up her big old ass. I had to laugh to myself thinking about that scene, but I made sure not to laugh too loud. I wanted that next chip.

When I think about the staff at the hospital, Dr. Mays definitely stands out. I remember a couple of the aides that worked there, too. Clyde France and Mr. Bennet both worked the evening shift and there were rumors that both of them took the job to get out of being drafted.

Clyde was a tall, lanky guy with hair that was a little long. He was a pretty mellow guy, and although he had to enforce the rules, he wouldn't be a jerk about it.

Mr. Bennet, on the other hand, was a shorter guy who was trying really hard to be a badass. He didn't let us use his first name and sometimes it seemed like he was getting off on enforcing the rules, immediately sending you to the Quiet Room if he caught you smoking in the TV room.

In 1970 everyone smoked inside the building, which just added another layer to the stench of the place. We only got in trouble for being too young to smoke. So on top of the misery of seeing people who were shaking and screaming and getting into fights, we had to worry about this guy on a power trip about us breaking the rules. Maybe he would have been happier in Vietnam.

After being in classes all day, we would go to the Multi-purpose room. For three days a week we had group therapy, but the other days we could do stuff that was fun. There was a gym where we could shoot hoops or play games, and a stage where we put on little plays. Most of us wanted to go to the pool. There was one kid who came to Dammasch a few months after I arrived, named Scott Johnson.

Scott was a year or two younger than I was, and I guess he was a little depressed. He seemed pretty normal though, and the two of us hit it off. There was a level system at Dammasch, where you were given cards with different colors. Orange Level was the one with the most freedom. If you had an orange card you could roam around the property of the hospital on your own. Yellow Level was directly below orange and if you had a yellow card, you could go with another kid that had an orange card. Scott and I were pretty good at working the levels and would either have yellow or orange most of the time so we could go for little walks around the property. Sometimes we would go to this old shed where we would smoke cigarettes that we had sneaked off the unit from older patients.

Everyone started calling us The Scott Brothers because my last name was Scott and his first name was Scott. I knew what it was like to have a real brother and chasing around with Scott, punching each other and horsing around, felt familiar. It felt a little bit like Lee.

One night Scott woke me up. It was around 1:30 a.m.

"Jesse. Wake up. I'm hungry, are you hungry? Do you have anything to eat? Any stashed candy bars or anything?"

It took me a second to wake up.

"No. I'm out."

"OK, now listen, I think I know a way to get into the kitchen. Are you up for an adventure?" He winked at me.

I was always up for an adventure. Clyde and Mr. Bennett had gone home for the night, and there was one night guard who sat at the nurse's station. I can't remember his name, but I remember him being a big guy. We got down on our hands and knees and scooted along the floor as if we were in *Mission Impossible* or something. My heart was beating fast, and every time Scott and I looked at each other we would try to stifle our giggles as we made our way past the ward office, through the living room, and into the dining room.

The door to the kitchen was locked, of course, as was the metal partition that covered the buffet. There was another, smaller metal door that held the trays, though, and the lock on the panel behind the trays appeared to be broken. It was a way in. We quietly removed the trays, and somehow removed that back barrier without making enough sound to attract attention.

The space was small, about two feet by three feet, and maybe four feet deep. We slid our young bodies through and went on in, opening up the fridge and finding a huge stash of cookies. We started eating them, shoving them into our mouths as well as our pajamas, trying to save as many as we could carry for later. A little milk would have gone great with the cookies, but not the powdered stuff they served us in the hospital. We were giggling and chewing and our brains were temporarily filled with a rush of sugar and satisfaction. We didn't realize that by leaving the space where we had snuck in open, the light from the refrigerator was shining through that opening.

We heard the keys in the lock and looked at each other with wide eyes. We raced toward the opening to escape, and were caught red-handed. Obviously we had to give back all the cookies, and we each picked up double chores. We were grateful it wasn't Mr. Bennett who caught us though, and I still think it was worth it.

One day after school, we went swimming in the pool, doing back flips off the board. Afterward, we went into the locker room to shower and change. I remember being with Scott in the shower. There was nothing sexual about it at all, even though we were both naked. We were just talking and laughing, and when we were done with our shower, we just sat down on the floor and kept talking, letting the water continue to fall on us. I remember feeling all this warmth and comfort.

Lee and I never hung out in the shower together at home or anything, but it was like being with someone who understood me in a place that wasn't the hospital. There weren't any aids around when we went to the pool, which is pretty strange, given how a kid could actually hurt themselves pretty easily in the water. It's just another example of how things didn't make a lot of sense when I look back on it. Scott only stayed at Dammasch for two or three months, and I really missed him when he left.

I had another experience in the multipurpose room that wasn't supervised. I got laid by an actual girl! There was a teenager there named Melissa who I later found out was in the hospital because she was a nymphomaniac. Is that even a real thing? I don't know all the terms for mental health issues that we use today, but Melissa was definitely really into sex.

I was in the gym area and she was up on the stage, peeking her head out behind the curtain. She signaled for me to come join her, so I looked around to make sure no one was watching and I hopped up on stage.

When I stepped behind the curtain, I saw that Melissa was stark naked. She looked at me and said, "Just do me!" And so I did. It was quick, it was nondescript, and even though I was able to go through the mechanics, it wasn't something I enjoyed that much. Nothing to write home about. (As if I would ever share that with my family besides Lee.) Mostly I just wished Scott was still there so I could tell him about it.

After Scott left, I started hanging out with this older guy named Mark who was in my unit. He didn't have a bed in the pod, but he was in one of the private rooms down the hall that could be locked. Mark was in his thirties, and also seemed pretty normal. We would play cards together a lot and watch TV. He would always give me cigarettes that I would go smoke in the shed when I had an orange card. I thought he was a pretty nice guy, even if he was a lot older.

One day, Mark asked if I wanted to play cards in his room. We were in there for a little while when he suggested we play strip poker. I hadn't ever played it before, but I was bored and thought it might make the game more interesting.

Well, I was only 13 and Mark was a much better poker player than I was, and before long I was totally naked. I think Mark had maybe taken off his shirt, but I had clearly been the one to lose all my clothes. Mark had this weird look on his face and he scooched over a little closer and put his hand on my leg. I thought that was weird. We started to play another hand and Mark said, "You know, Jesse, you don't have anything else to take off, and seeing as how you lost, I think it would only be fair if you let me touch your privates. You want the game to be fair don't you?"

Now remember, this was 1970. We didn't have talks about Stranger Danger or Healthy Boundaries or anything like that. All I knew was that I lost at poker and now this guy wants to touch my penis.

"I mean, I guess. If those are the rules."

Well, he touched it and he started to move his head down towards it, and an aid walked by and saw what was going on. The next thing I know they are yelling at me to get my clothes on. I scrambled as fast as I could because they were really yelling at me. A little later I saw Mark being led away in handcuffs. I guess Mark had a history of doing that sort of thing, which was why he was in a private room in the first place.

I was pretty scared that I was going to get into trouble. I was pulled into an office and asked again and again why I went into his room. I was fully expecting them to drop my level or something, but instead they moved all the adults out of the private rooms and moved all the kids into them.

At first the other kids were really annoyed because it meant we were by ourselves at night. They didn't know about me and Mark, and I didn't share it with anyone. I just took this as my punishment for going into his room.

After a while, we got used to the private rooms and the kids were actually pretty happy about it. I still didn't take credit for it though, because even though I wanted that attention, I knew the thing that happened between me and Mark was wrong. Mark ended up returning from jail several weeks later and he was placed back onto our unit. That was awkward. He tried to get me to let him into my room but I knew better this time. When he was finally released he left me a note that said that I should meet him on the edge of the property so we could be together. I threw it in the garbage.

After the incident with Mark, Dr. Mays decided I needed a new responsibility. She would have me leave class to walk down the glass hallway to the reception desk so I could check the thermometer and barometer. I would then return to class and give a report on the weather. I would take my time, goofing off on my way down the hall, sometimes taking up to a half hour before returning back to the class. I would do my best TV Weatherman impression, and I would hear the sound of two chips falling, *clink clink*.

I'm not sure if she felt sorry for me or if she just realized that I was the smartest 8th grader she had, and that I needed something new for my brain to focus on each day. Maybe she just had hopes for my future career in meteorology. I know that for that half hour each school day, I experienced a little more freedom and a little more purpose. I really liked Dr. Mays.

I remember watching as the other kids left with their parents for day visits. Saturdays were usually the worst days at the hospital. Each week, on Wednesdays, during Process Group, kids would vote on who got to visit family that week. It wasn't like there was a limited number of slots. All of them could have a visit if they earned it. But to earn it, you had to get the approval of your peers. Besides being on the right level and having earned enough points, you had to show that you were "taking accountability for yourself," and "positively contributing to the community of the milieu," and obviously you were "not a run risk" or "a threat to yourself or others."

Each of the kids in the unit were able to vote to support their peers in being able to have a visit, or could vote to send a message that a kid needed to be trying harder. The kids actually took it seriously and voted based on how you were behaving and not just on your level of popularity.

I remember one particular weekend I had Rocked the Vote on Wednesday, and on Saturday, I had my backpack ready for my visit. I had a sweatshirt in case it got cold, and a God's Eye I'd made for my mom in a crafts group. I had a paper I'd written on WWI I thought my dad might like to read. I had a poster of Black Sabbath I'd traded something for and I thought Lee might like, even though I doubted my parents would bring Lee. They never brought Lee to the hospital. They told me Lee was too young, even though he was only ten months younger than me, and at age thirteen I actually lived at the hospital. If Lee wasn't there, they could give him the poster when they got home. Hopefully we could go to Shakey's Pizza again. I thought I might order Canadian Bacon this time. I could even start to smell it.

As the morning wore on, and more kids left the unit, I tried to ignore the familiar knot that was forming in my stomach. I watched TV hoping to be distracted as I waited. The ads showing All American Families eating their cheese slices during their backyard barbecues didn't help. It was hard to believe that wasn't everyone's life. Everyone in the real world.

The knot started to move up into my chest as the day went along, making it feel both tight and hollow. The thoughts started coming in too. *I'm a piece of shit. I'm not normal. If I was normal I wouldn't be here. If I was their real kid they'd come get me. If only I liked girls.*

I tried to use some of the skills I had been taught here. Replace those thoughts with other, more rational explanations. *Maybe Lee had a game today. Maybe the car broke down. Maybe mom isn't feeling well.* Those just felt like excuses though. Even though my parents had said "we'll see…" I knew deep down they weren't really coming. It was the fifth Saturday in a row.

By early afternoon, the lump in my throat felt rock-solid and sometimes I would start to cry. This brought on new thoughts. *Oh, look at the faggot crying. Why can't you be a man?*

The aids would try to help, but the more attention they gave me, the worse I felt. I knew they were getting paid to be there. I knew they wouldn't ever let me visit their homes. I also knew that compared to the other patients who were screaming or actively trying to kill themselves, my crying about not visiting my family wasn't a priority for them.

As the evening rolled in and the kids returned, I started making jokes. I created rich fantasy visits that involved private airplanes and extravagant meals. It was a running joke, and helped everyone laugh along with me. The word "pathetic" kept rolling around my head, but as long as I could make a joke, it had less power.

I didn't know it yet, but the following Thursday I would not be approved for a visit. It's not that my peers didn't think I'd earned it. They just couldn't bear to watch me go through it every week.

I found out later that my parents had actually gone to the Department of Human Services and petitioned the court to have me made a Ward of the State. Basically, it means they un-adopted me. Kind of like if you adopt an animal from the Humane Society and it is too much to handle, you can bring it back and let someone else deal with it. I guess the hospital was going to have to figure out what to do with me instead of my parents. Beyond a day visit home to celebrate Christmas, where I was given a watch that I couldn't bring back to the hospital, I never got to go home. After a few months my parents stopped pretending to visit, and I stopped getting my hopes up. I know most teenagers think they don't have a lot of control in their lives, but for my situation it was next-level.

Every morning I woke up and the first thought I had was "I wonder what fresh hell will happen today?" Most teenagers were worried about zits and dating and grades. I was worried that I would see someone actually kill themselves. God knows I saw people try it in all kinds of creative ways: slitting their wrists, trying to hang themselves, throwing themselves down concrete stairs. Those folks would be sent to the medical part of the hospital and then brought back, sometimes with visible scars. To this day, when I hear about suicide, it takes me back to Dammasch. How ironic that this place I mostly associated with fear, was the place my parents sent me to get better.

A couple of weeks after the thing with Mark happened, I decided I was done being at Dammasch. I had been there for six or seven months and I asked my friend Denise if she wanted to run away with me. I had an orange card and she had a yellow card, so I could be her escort off the ward and onto the property. Once we hit the edge of the property we had to decide if we should take the roads away from Dammasch or run through the fields. We thought the roads would be easier, but we would also be easier to spot once they figured out we had been gone too long. We decided to run through the fields. Unfortunately, we didn't realize that within the fields there was a slough.

We took off our shoes and socks and stepped into the water to cross over to the other side. The water was really slimy and smelly and it came up to my waist. Denise waded in and it came up to her chest. I remember walking through that squishy mud, covered in filth, feeling like I was escaping from prison. I climbed out and started to put my shoes and socks on when I heard Denise start screaming to high heaven.

"Oh my God Jesse! Oh my God! Help me!"

I looked over and she was covered in leeches. Shit. I looked all over my own body and luckily I didn't have any on me, so I tried to help calm her down.

"It's OK. Let me just pick them off."

"Jesse, they're all over me. That hurts. Are they sucking my blood? Am I going to have blood left? This is so gross I can't stand it."

I tried to be patient while picking them off of her.

"Listen, calm down. You're not going to die. Maybe you're just sweeter than I am and that's why they're all over you and not on me."

She rolled her eyes, but it did help her to calm down a little bit. I really wanted to throw up, but I didn't want her to freak out even more than she was already.

We followed the railroad tracks for a while in the direction of Portland, and eventually made it out of the town of Wilsonville. We agreed to go to the interstate and start hitchhiking. It took forever to get a ride. A few people pulled over and let us get in, but once they smelled us stinking like the slough they kicked us out of their car. Eventually a guy gave us a ride all the way into downtown Portland and dropped us off. We looked at each other and realized that we didn't have any money, or food, or a place to stay. It was starting to get dark and we didn't really know what to do. We decided to panhandle for some change until we got enough money to go into Fogelman's Diner, a place that was open late, maybe all night. Even though we really wanted cheeseburgers, we only had enough money for coffee.

Denise and I had clearly not thought out this plan, and the reality of our situation sunk in. Neither of us could call our family to have them come pick us up. We didn't know anyone else to call, and it was getting dark and cold. We finally made the decision to call the hospital so that they could come pick us up.

Man, we felt really pathetic. I mean, looking back I guess it was an adventure. The sadness really hit hard that day though, because the reality of my situation came crashing down on my fantasy of being able to escape. I could escape the physical location of the hospital, but I couldn't escape the fact that no one wanted to help me. No one was there for me. I was trapped, and I felt utterly alone.

Some of these memories make me smile. I mean, leeches and shower chats and a quickie behind the curtain. But someone was always yelling or moaning or screaming or shaking. There was always someone pounding on the door of the Quiet Room, the loudest room on the unit. I would watch people walk back from receiving shock therapy, wondering if I would be next. My mother let me know that because of my history with seizures she'd made sure that the hospital would never give me shock therapy. I didn't trust this at the time though, so it was just one more thing that was confusing and scary. It usually smelled like urine or feces, with a layer of disinfectant on top to cover it up. I knew it was a dangerous place, and I learned I shouldn't be alone, except when I was alone at night in my private room. It was the most painful year of my life. Dammit, now I am starting to shake, and if I don't get out of this space the tears will come next.

As if on cue, Lee's finally calling me back and he is even acting a little interested in the information I've found. He had some choice words to say about the ethnicity part, even saying that maybe our mom was a whore after all. I know that Lee has his own way of protecting himself. I think about the lasting impact that Dammasch had on me and I was only there for a year. Lee was incarcerated for a total of 22 years. It's kind of amazing that he is as normal as he is right now. I mean, he's pretty rough and he comes out swinging when presented with a challenge. He's covered in tattoos, but these days so is everyone else. I have teased him about being a Portland Hipster and he just tells me to fuck off. With the way Lee dresses, you would never think he was anything but a biker.

Like usual, Lee's happy to have me take the lead on this search. I don't think he has the patience for it or the ability to handle more disappointment. Obviously I don't tell him this. He's working all the time now, and I'm not, and so I tell him that I have time to look into it. He also made a joke about the name Marty Dick and about how much I love dicks. It's meaner when he says it, but I'm used to it. We agree that I will let him know when I find something out, but unless I actually find our mom or dad, I won't make it sound like an emergency.

Maybe I can start my own poker chip system. Every time I get a clue and refrain from completely freaking out I can reward myself. Instead of poker chips I can use cigarettes and candy. If nothing else, the deep breathing of a cigarette won't hurt.

Chapter 8

Level One

It's been a full week since I opened my results from Ancestry and I'm still waiting to hear back from Marty Dick. I got a message that said that Marty Dick wasn't actually the person who signed up for Ancestry—it was her daughter who did it on her behalf. Well, her daughter wasn't about to tell me anything, but she did let me know that her mom just got married and is on a cruise. I guess she'll be back in a few days.

It would be great to find out she was on one of the same boats John and I traveled on when we went on our cruises. So far we've gone to Mexico and through the Panama Canal. We love cruises, because you get to meet all these great people and go on exciting excursions without all the hassle of making the arrangements yourself. Maybe I can start the conversation with Marty talking about cruise ships and she will be more relaxed. If she didn't even sign up for Ancestry herself, I can assume she won't be enthusiastic about talking to a stranger who wants information about her family.

I start my job next week working for Christopher. He's 19 and was in a swimming accident in the Pacific Ocean. He's a quadriplegic and so will need a lot of help. I'll be driving to Laguna Beach and staying there for five days a week. Apparently, it's a big house and they have an area for me to stay in. I'm not expecting something fancy, but am hoping it's comfortable. I know that not all caregivers are rewarded for the hard work of taking on the intimate tasks that are more difficult and awkward for the actual family to perform. I'm not sure why that is, but it's the same with nurses and teachers and lots of jobs that have historically been done by women. Not every situation is going to end up actually feeling like family. I think I was just spoiled working for Jim and Milan.

I am looking forward to seeing the ocean again, but don't know how this new arrangement will impact my relationship with John. I'm hoping that having a little space will help him appreciate me more. It's not that he doesn't love me, I know he does, but sometimes it feels like we're roommates more than romantic partners. After so many years together I know that's normal. If someone would have told me thirty years ago that I would be part of an old married couple I would've told them they were nuts. I know he won't mind me earning some money again. It's been nice having all this time off though.

In the meantime, I am trying to clean up this house. Earlier this morning I spent some time dusting and it was pretty obvious that chore was overdue. We have so many trinkets all over this house, it's a little ridiculous. My mom gave me a curio cabinet when I was in Portland that has been my favorite piece of furniture. It's full of fancy things, like crystal candlesticks, and little figurines. There are even some vases and little dishes that we collected on our travels. John likes to say they are dust collectors, but he has just as much crap as I do, and I am the one that usually does most of the dusting. Some of this stuff might be worth some money, but I like them because they look nice. I have to remind John that I didn't always get to keep nice stuff.

After living at the hospital for a year, they finally sent me to a residential program called St. Mary's Home for Boys. The staff at St. Mary's looked through my stuff as they checked me into the program. They wrote down all my inventory and told me about the levels. There were six, apparently, and they involved earning points.

I nodded and thought, "This just sounds like the level system and chip thing at the hospital all over again."

At St. Mary's, though, it seemed like it took more time to climb your way up. For example, on Level 1 you were given a card every morning and there were time slots with numbers next to them. The staff had hole punches, and every half hour they would punch the number that correlated to your behavior. You had to get a certain number of points to make an average, and to go to Level 2, you had to "make average" every day for three weeks straight. That seemed a little extreme. If you messed up at the end of week two, you had to go back to the beginning.

When you reached Level 2, you were given a card each day, but instead of rating your behavior every half-hour, it was every hour. Again, you had to make average every day for three weeks to reach Level 3. The time slots widened with each level you advanced.

When you reached Level 5, the time slots went away and you were judged for breakfast, chores, school, and evening. You could also go off grounds with someone else, just like at the hospital.

On Level 6, you didn't have a card at all, you were just given a pass/fail. On Level 6 you could leave the property on your own, and take the bus or walk to shops. St. Mary's wasn't so far out in the middle of nowhere, but was in a small suburb of Portland called Aloha. It's pronounced Uh-low-uh, not like the Hawaiian word. It's not a bad place, but it's definitely not Hawaii.

I sat listening to the staff explain the levels, and did some quick math in my head to figure out how quickly I could get up to Level 5 and 6. I knew that was where I could experience a little freedom and independence. It sounded like I wouldn't need to run away from this place to get it.

The staff took me to my room and told me I could get settled in. The room was neon orange and smelled as if it had been freshly painted. There was a bed, and a night stand and a little dresser. I put away my stuff, and then sat on the edge of the bed, waiting.

The staff told me that there would be a whistle, and I would be expected to stand outside my door to be counted. When I emerged from my room I realized that I was the only boy there who had his own single room. Everyone else was given a room with two or three guys with bunk beds. I didn't know if it was because I had come from the hospital or because I was gay.

It's funny though, when you think about it. You put the gay kid in the hospital because he was gay, and now you're going to send him to a place called St. Mary's Home For Boys? I mean, yes, please.

The other boys didn't seem to connect that I had the single room for that reason, and I didn't make a big deal out of it. It was just something I noticed that, again, made me different. I actually spotted a kid that I recognized from the hospital. I always thought he was gay, but he never came out and told people and I never said anything to him directly. I think it was just my gaydar going off, even if that word didn't exist back then. He had roommates at St. Mary's, which let me know he was still keeping his sexual orientation under wraps. Beyond a subtle nod, he didn't make a big deal about recognizing me, and so I didn't either.

I immediately understood the change in population. I was finally in a place where everyone was a kid. There was an elementary program there but they were in another house and we only saw them in passing on our way to school. The kids at St. Mary's were different from the kids at the hospital. They were less likely to be fragile or to be struggling with mental health issues, and more likely to be kids who were acting out.

Most of the kids were in the foster care system and were sent there for things like stealing, skipping too much school, fighting, or impulse control. To be honest, it was a breath of fresh air. I wasn't constantly worried about finding someone who had killed themselves or adults trying to grope me. There was no electric shock treatment either.

I concentrated on the level system with laser focus and made it straight through to Level 5 without a day where I didn't make my average. For once, I was the good kid. Well, usually I was the good kid. That didn't mean I couldn't have fun.

One day I was sitting in science class waiting for Sister Delores to arrive. I turned to the guys sitting near me and looked like I had a secret. "Hey you guys, do you know why Sister Delores is a nun?"

"Oh shit….why, Jesse?" They leaned in to hear the punchline.

"Because she ain't had none. She ain't gonna get none…." I went on and on as everyone around me was totally cracking up.

Suddenly, though, the room got really quiet and I realized the boys weren't looking at me anymore, they were looking behind me. Looking at Sister Delores, as she stood behind me with her hands on her hips. Clearly I messed up my points pretty bad, but we all had a good laugh. I was always getting a good laugh.

There was a little forested area out back that had the different stations of the cross. The nuns would go out there to pray, and once you hit Level 5 you could go out there too. We would hide cigarettes in the bushes and sneak smokes when we knew the nuns wouldn't be around. Sometimes the nuns would do a sweep, though, and you would discover they had thrown away your smokes. I guess it could have been another kid taking them, but we always blamed the nuns. I wonder if they were smoking them somewhere in their own private place?

There was one woman who worked there who was a former nun. I can't remember her name, but I do remember she was in her twenties and had long dark hair. She was very pretty, and a lot of the boys had crushes on her. She didn't put up with much, though, and I remember her saying very sternly, "Just because I am a woman here, that doesn't mean you get to act up around me." She was as stern as a nun, but without the habit.

Father Stevens was the main guy in charge, and his office was right next to the entrance of one of the houses where we lived. Kids mostly ended up there when they were in trouble. There was a dining hall and a living room on that floor too. I was thrilled with the difference in the food. Finally, we had real whole milk. No more of that powdered junk. The food was also geared more towards kids. We had weenies and beans, sandwiches, burgers. I'm not sure why the hospital food was so heavy and boiled to death, but this felt more like food that teenagers would eat. There wasn't a pool, but there was a ping pong table in the living room, and overall, the place just smelled so much better. I mean, it still smelled like a bunch of teenage boys, which is actually pretty gross, but that's better than smelling like the hospital. I guess at that point my standards were low.

There was a lot more freedom at St. Mary's than at the hospital. One day, when I made Level 6, I walked into downtown Beaverton to check it out. There was a pet shop, and I went in to look around. I spotted a really cute little hamster and it reminded me of the one that Lee owned as a kid. Lee named that hamster "Lunch" because one time our cat tried to eat it. Lunch was pretty cute and soft, and I thought that sounded like a nice addition to my room. I had earned some money and so I bought the hamster, a cage, a wheel, some bark chips, and some food. I walked back to St. Mary's feeling so excited to show the other kids. I wondered why no one else thought of buying a pet.

Well, when I walked in with it, the staff just looked at me like I was nuts. Of course you couldn't have pets at St Mary's. I don't know what I was thinking. Father Stevens let me have it in my room for one night, but then it had to go away. I didn't name it because I didn't want to get too attached. I had yet to get a visit from my parents or Lee, and I knew the danger of getting attached. I think I just got carried away and for an afternoon I let myself believe I could do something normal like have a pet. Like have hope.

When I reached Level 6, I was able to leave the campus and attend regular school. I was in 9th grade and attended Mountain View Junior High, which was within walking distance from St. Mary's.

I remember going into the school on my first day; the school year was well under way. I wonder if the teachers at St. Mary's had pushed for me to go, even though it was the middle of the semester, because they could tell how bored I was in class at the facility.

I walked into math class and they happened to be having a quiz. It was a Friday, I don't remember why I started on a Friday, but I was expected to take the quiz even though it was my first day. Well, I tried to do my best on that quiz but I ended up getting an F. I was devastated. I loved math and always thought that it came pretty easily.

I spent the weekend worried that my bad grade might make the school send me back, as if it had been a mistake to send me there in the first place. Instead of giving in to all those doubts, I took that grade and used it as incentive to actually study. I loved being at a normal school so much I didn't want to get sent home for something like bad grades.

Well, I ended up getting A's on all the weekly math quizzes, and overall I ended up being a good student academically. I loved science class, and really got into it on the day we had to dissect a frog. Some of the other kids thought it was gross, or mean to the frogs, but I found it fascinating. It felt so good to be back in a public school. I don't remember the other kids asking if I was from St. Mary's. I wasn't volunteering that information. There were a couple of other boys from the facility who were able to go to that school, too, and we didn't necessarily hang out with each other, which was fine with me. I saw them all the time.

Finally, I could separate school from treatment, and I loved the break from having staff constantly evaluate my behavior. I still missed going to school with my brother though, even if we weren't in the same grade and had different friends. It was comforting to know he was close by.

I didn't get to see Lee when I moved to St. Mary's, but we did talk on the phone. It was only good if he was in a place where my parents couldn't hear what he was saying. He had a lot of complaints about them, and I think they thought that if I agreed with him then it was my fault that they weren't getting along.

Lee told me recently he felt kind of bad because he knew if he kept playing sports and doing things that made it obvious to my parents he wasn't gay, then he could keep doing other stuff like skipping school and smoking pot.

I don't think he liked being the only kid at home now that Sis was long gone. I hadn't been home for over a year. He still had his dog, Angel, but clearly she wasn't as much fun as me. Sometimes I would exaggerate all the cool stuff we got to do at St. Mary's, and I don't know if that made Lee feel bad or not. I just knew that I was trying to make the best of my situation and sometimes we did end up doing some cool stuff.

The Portland Trail Blazers had some sort of arrangement with St. Mary's, so the basketball players would come every few months to shoot hoops with us. They even gave us tickets to see Blazer games at the Memorial Coliseum in Portland. To this day, I am a diehard Blazers fan.

The Jaycees liked to volunteer at St. Mary's too, and each winter if you were on Level 6 you could go skiing once a week up at Mt. Hood for six weeks. They had a big van and would pick us up early in the morning. We would drive up to the mountain, which was a couple hours away, rent our gear, and hit the slopes. They gave us basic skiing lessons, but once you conquered the bunny hill, you were on your own. I absolutely loved it. I felt so free gliding down the mountain with all that snow, and the view from the top.

Even though I fell a lot, It felt so peaceful up there—which I guess was the whole point. There were staff to watch the kids that struggled, but if you could ski on your own, you only had to worry about being back at Timberline lodge by 4 p.m.

One day I was skiing, and I got back to the lodge at 3:30 p.m. I remember looking at my watch and realizing that I only had a half hour, and I knew that I would never make it down in time if I did a final run. I gave it some thought—for about a minute—and then I headed to the ski lift and made my way up.

Well, of course I was about thirty minutes late, and the staff were not happy at all, so I had to miss skiing the next week. Fortunately, that happened in week four, so even though I missed week five, I still had one more trip before the end of the season. Now that I think about it, I traded one hour of skiing for a whole day. That's so dumb. I'm not sure if it was impulsivity, or just the way the teenage brain works, but at the time, I didn't regret it much. Delayed gratification is hard.

I just talked to Marty Dick. She wasn't that helpful, to be honest, and she definitely seemed a little suspicious of me, even if I did let her tell me all about her cruise.

Marty told me that she had gotten sober several years ago and had basically cut herself off from the Hurst side of her family to try to stay that way. I am trying not to take that as a red flag, but I admit it's making me a little nervous. I'm not in recovery or anything, as I still enjoy a cocktail or a glass of wine with one of the meals John makes me. I haven't used meth for years though, and I know what a relief it is to be out of that life, where everyone around you is a tweaker and the focus of your attention is always on the next high.

I remember how bad I was when I lived in San Francisco. I was in my twenties, and I admit my life had pretty well spiraled out of control. I'd lost whatever job I had at the time, and I was about to lose my apartment. I had just gone on a huge binge, shooting up meth and snorting some coke. I didn't know it, but my dad had driven down to pick me up, kind of like a one man intervention.

I tried to tell him I was busy, but he wouldn't go away, and instead he just stood there watching me try to throw some of my stuff in a suitcase so that he could drive me back to Portland. Talk about a long drive!

Seriously, though, if I think about how irritated and frustrated I felt trying to pretend like I wasn't completely spinning, I imagine it was more uncomfortable for my dad, especially since I couldn't help with the driving. I'm sure he was sick of listening to me babble non stop. I should try to remember this the next time I get upset with my dad. He didn't have to do that, I suppose. It's too bad that it didn't stick. I still used drugs once I got back to Portland.

Marty said she didn't know Donna Hurst, but she did end up giving me a phone number for her cousin, Lorraine. I already called Lorraine and left her a voicemail. Even though I lost my mind a little with excitement when I first heard back from Ancestry, I have been feeling calmer. There is this painting that John brought with him when he moved in that is hanging on the wall next to the computer. It's a mix of oranges and blues, and even though it's abstract, you can make out some figures. There is a big sun, an eagle, a feather, and a Native American. I'm guessing the person is male, because he has a couple of feathers in his hair, but his features are not clear and, like I said, it's kind of abstract. Can Native American women wear feathers? I thought I read somewhere that feathers were associated with being a warrior. I know I sound really ignorant. I don't know the history behind the painting, but it feels soothing, and it's definitely healthier than the American Spirit I am about to smoke. Thinking about tweaking and about St. Mary's brings up more memories that even this painting can't soothe away.

I was still at St. Mary's in 1971 when Father Stevens brought me to his office to talk to me about a possible foster home. It was a man, Merle Doyle, who had a home with boys in it. Apparently, it was not another place like the hospital or St. Mary's, but an actual home, and it had a pool in the backyard and everything. He told me that I could continue to go to the high school I was attending, but at Merle's home I would have built-in brothers. Merle was supposed to be a great guy, and after reading about me, he thought he might like to meet me.

I was definitely interested. I had seen so many boys come and go in the time I had been there. Kids who responded to the level system and didn't seem so out of control. They had all gone back to their own homes or to a new foster home. A lot of kids had actually come from foster care before St. Mary's and were going back, and the way they described it, it all sounded like it depended on who the foster parents were. Not much different than real parents, I thought. Luck seemed to have a lot to do with how it all turned out. It seemed pretty lucky to get a foster home with a pool. Lee would be so jealous! What did I have to lose? My parents were clear that I wasn't coming home. I had stopped asking.

"That's great! Merle usually takes his new boys on a camping trip to see if they'll fit in with the group. He wants to pick you up on Friday after school." Father Stevens stood up, signaling that the meeting was over. "This could be a great opportunity for you Jesse. Please don't mess it up, OK?"

We sat around the campfire as Merle told ghost stories. The other boys were rolling their eyes and groaning, but were good sports about it. We had eaten hot dogs for dinner and were roasting marshmallows. I still remembered my technique for getting marshmallows done "just the right amount" from all our camping trips at the beach. The other boys seemed a little surprised to hear that I had gone on beach trips with my family before I ended up locked up. The other boys didn't talk a lot about their parents.

I was used to sleeping in a tent with Lee while our parents had their own tent. Merle had a huge tent though, and he and the other boys would all be there together. Roger, the oldest boy, was at one end of the tent. Mick, the second oldest, was beside him. Then was Jimmy, who was three days older than me but a year behind in school. Then Merle, then me on the other end of the tent.

I always had a little trouble falling asleep in new places, but I loved sleeping outside, and I drifted off as the sounds of the crickets and the smell of the campfire seeped through the tent. I woke up to a hand reaching inside my sleeping bag. I jumped, but heard Merle whispering in my ear to be quiet. To not wake up the others. My body tensed. I could feel Merle's hand reaching around my sweatpants until he found what he wanted. I didn't move. I didn't want to wake the others and have them find out what was going on. What I was doing.

Before Merle rolled over, he whispered in my ear, "If you say anything to anybody, well, they already know you're a faggot. You've been in the hospital. Who do you think they are going to believe? Me or you?"

Father Stevens brought me into his office to hear about the camping trip.

"Well, Jesse? I hear from Merle that he thinks you will make an excellent addition to his home. Congratulations, son!" Father Stevens was beaming. "You look tired. I bet you had a great time on the trip! That was so kind of him to take you camping."

I sat in the chair and nodded. I couldn't believe this was happening. After all the work with the chips and the levels and now I had to go live with this pervert. It was true though, they would never believe a 14-year-old faggot who had been in a mental hospital. Everyone seemed to think this guy, Merle, was the best foster parent around. Maybe he just did this to me this one time because he had heard about me. Maybe it could be like a normal home, or at least as much of a normal home as some fucked up, no good queer kid could expect?

"Well, Jesse, what do you think? Is it a plan?"

I swallowed and nodded my head. "Yes. It's a plan."

Now my stomach is starting to hurt thinking of this stuff. Big breath. I need to get myself together for this new job, which might be a good thing to focus on right now. I guess I only need to bring clothing for five days, my hygiene stuff or as John would say all my "fancy hair products," and a few packs of cigarettes. Maybe after I work for a while I can buy myself a laptop. I have a computer that I use that is a whole contraption of wires that I obviously need to keep here. I guess I can use my phone to keep checking Ancestry and to keep playing Farmville on Facebook. We'll see if I have as much of a computer addiction as John thinks I have by being forced to take a break. There better be a TV in my little room. I can't be expected to do something desperate like read a book or something.

It's kind of amazing, really, that here I am taking care of a kid with major disabilities who is a complete stranger. He will need to trust me at such a primal level—to give him his meds and to wipe his butt and every other intimate act you can imagine. His mom will need to trust me in their home, wherever I end up sleeping.

John needed to trust me when he first moved in with his abstract painting and cooking supplies. Thinking back to these memories about getting dropped off at Dammasch, and about going to Merle's house—how is it that I can trust anyone? How did I become so trustworthy?

Years ago I worked at Cascade AIDS Project as a housing case manager. I was good at that job, not only because I had really good boundaries and could see through the people we served who were addicts, because I gained their trust.

This cousin, Lorraine, will hopefully trust me and eventually I can meet my biological mom, Donna. I tried to talk to John about it and he listened and then said in his matter of fact way, "Yes, Jesse, they will learn to trust you. How will you know if you can trust them?"

Chapter 9

My "Beard"

I wish I could say that I moved in with Merle and that he never touched me again. I wish I could say that when he did touch me again, I told my DHS caseworker and had him arrested, and I went to go live with my parents and Lee again. I wish I could say that the first time Merle made me go into his room and look at porn, and then do things that I don't want to spell out here, that I could have kicked him in that ugly old dick of his or called him a dirty pervert or anything, really. Of course I didn't, just like most kids don't, and instead I just figured out ways to stay out of the house.

Merle's house was pretty big and did indeed have a pool. Merle was married to Dot, and it was strange because Dot slept in a bedroom downstairs while Merle slept upstairs in a bedroom closer to us boys. Roger was the oldest and he was Dot's biological son, and he slept in the garage that had been converted to a bedroom. Jimmy and I shared a room, and Mick had his own room.

Dot was very quiet and was a few years older than Merle. I think she was an accountant or something, so she would get up and go to work and then spend the rest of her time in her room watching TV. She had an older daughter, Susan, who would come over and not hide her feelings for Merle. I didn't know why she hated him so much, but she would always be really rude to him, and Merle wouldn't do anything about it.

Susan was a beautician, so she would bring over all these fancy hair products. One time I tried to secretly dye my hair blonde using some of her hair dye, but it didn't take. I have no idea why I thought I could hide it if it did actually turn blonde.

I think about my time at Merle's, and the word that comes to mind is "misery." I had so much experience living with other kids, but in some ways, having three built-in siblings was harder than living among a bigger group of kids. They were all really into going to the gym, and occasionally they would drag me along. I would bring a book and sit in a corner while they lifted weights. They would always pick at me, calling me names and pointing out how much of a wimp I was while they were all so tough. Jimmy was especially annoying, constantly slugging my shoulder and giving me shit. You would think it would remind me of Lee, but it was different. There wasn't the underlying bond or love that I had with Lee. Instead it just made me feel isolated.

On top of going to a different school and having different interests, I also assumed that I was the only one that Merle was bothering. I would be getting ready for school while the other boys were at the gym and I would hear Merle say, "Jesse, come in here." My heart would sink and the knot in my stomach would form instantly. I would come in and Merle would pull out one of his porno magazines and show me photos. He had magazines that were all men, and others that were men and women. He would ask me, "What's that doing for you?" while he undid his pants and started stroking himself. He would make me take off my pants and then he would do things to me or make me do things to him. I always felt disgusted while it was happening, and because I was 14 years old, my body would respond in ways I didn't want it to. I mean, at that age, I would get an erection if the wind blew in the right direction. I was constantly being called a sissy by the other boys, so I just assumed this was only happening to me. I also assumed that somehow I was causing this behavior, or at the least, I was not actively making it stop.

Even though I was trying my best to stay out of the house, it would happen two or three times a week. In some ways, I started thinking of it as one of my chores, like doing the dishes or cleaning the bathroom. I would have gladly traded that in for more chores, believe me. I'm guessing that if I'd been given double the chores instead of sexual abuse, I wouldn't have so much trouble being physically affectionate. Maybe I would actually enjoy having other people touch me.

I was sharing a room with Jimmy, who was my age, and I was trying to hide what was going on with Merle. Years later, I would meet up with Jimmy by chance at a gay bar and he told me Merle was doing the same thing to him, too. I have no idea how Merle was able to pull it off, without us hearing it or knowing it was going on. We agreed that the really gross part of it all—well, one of the gross parts of it all—was that Merle made us all call him "Dad." So on top of feeling gross about what was happening, there was this extra layer that felt incestuous. I don't hate many people, but I hate Merle with my whole soul. Still.

I was going to Adams High School, which was eventually called Fernhill. I think they tore it down, but the track is still there and now it's just a park. All the other boys went to a different high school, Benson, that was more focused on learning the trades. I wasn't able to go there because you couldn't transfer into it after your freshman year.

My school was actually pretty groovy. They had this experimental model that was open and you could have a little more freedom. I discovered theater, which I know isn't a big surprise, given how much I love attention. I joined the choir too. I was getting all A's in my performing arts class-es and D's and F's in my academic classes. It was a pretty big adjustment to go back to normal society after being locked up and on a points and levels system for so long, and I quickly figured out that if I skipped school, no one was going to come tackle me or give me consequences like I was used to at the hospital. I was also having a hard time focusing in the more serious classes, because I couldn't stop thinking about the stuff Merle was doing.

The other boys would all drive to their high school, and I would take the city bus. There was an older woman who drove that route, and my stop happened to be where she took her break. Sometimes she would be eating a sandwich or drinking coffee when I got on and we would end up chatting. I think she could tell there was something odd about me. I'm not sure if it was because it was obvious I didn't have any friends, or if it was just a vibe, but she was always really kind and went out of her way to chat with me and ask me about how my day was going.

After a while, I started to open up a little and I told her I wasn't happy living with Merle. I didn't tell her what was going on, and she didn't ask for details, but she did encour-age me to tell my DHS caseworker that I wanted to move. I think about her sometimes, and about how this woman I didn't even know thought that I deserved to be happy. Instead of taking her advice, I just continued to find excus-es to spend time away. I joined choir and drama, where I could be a part of a group of kids who wouldn't call me a sissy. That helped.

I ended up with a young woman named JoAn, who would become a type of a girlfriend. She was Mormon, and was pretty serious about her religion. I had no interest in having sex with a girl, and it was against her religion, so no one really questioned why we were mostly just friends.

She told me that Seminary Classes—what we would call Bible Study—were held every day before school, and that ended up giving me the perfect excuse to leave Merle's house early in the morning. I can't say I ended up believing everything, but it did provide a safe space to go and talk to God and let Him know what was going on.

JoAn's parents were pretty impressed by her nice boyfriend, and the Elders were thrilled that there was a young man open to the Church. It ended up taking time before school days, and most of the whole day on Sundays. After a while, the only day I was available to Merle was on Saturday. One or two days a week was better than three or four. It wasn't as satisfying as hurting Merle, but it was a way to protect myself.

I had never heard the word "beard" before, but I think it means something like having a pretend straight girlfriend so no one knows you are gay. JoAn was the perfect beard, and her church was the perfect place to get away from the house. I wonder whatever happened to her. I hope she ended up with a real straight man who was actually interested in her and her church, and not just using her to avoid having to be molested. She deserves that much.

I talked to Lee the other day, and told him about my new job working for Christopher in Laguna Beach. Lee has mostly done construction jobs and can't understand why I would be willing to "wipe some grown man's ass." I wonder what Lee would be like if he was really in that situation. I always tell people his bark is worse than his bite, and that he had to create this intense shell to survive being in prison for such a long time. Lee really is a softie underneath all his swearing and complaining, but clearly he would never qualify to be a caretaker given his criminal history, so I think that's why he kind of makes fun of the work I do sometimes.

Rosa is a case manager who inspects nursing homes, so she gets it and thinks it's great that I am doing this kind of work. I see Lee taking care of Rosa, especially now. I also see him taking care of his house and his dogs, and his biker brothers. If I ever told him directly, he'd probably tell me I was crazy, but I know it would secretly make him feel good.

Lee still doesn't seem too interested in my adventures with the Ancestry site, but my new client, Christopher, actually thinks it's pretty cool.

Christopher was adopted too, and he doesn't really feel the need to find his birth parents. He is more interested in figuring out his ethnicity. He keeps telling me to be careful about getting hurt, which is maybe what's holding him back from looking for his own biological family. So far, we're getting along pretty well. I'm staying in a room next to his so I can hear if he needs anything at night. My room doesn't have a TV, but once I pay off some bills, I'm thinking of buying one. The house is gorgeous, and the ocean is right there, and every weekend when I come back to the desert, John is waiting for me with a nice meal. I plop down on our worn out couch that I am sure Christopher's mom would find gross, but I can tell you it's more comfortable than their furniture. At least you don't have to worry about getting it dirty.

I left a voicemail for Lorraine Hurst, the woman who Marty Dick told me about. Apparently, Lorraine is the daughter of Donna's half brother, Sam. At least that's what Marty thinks. Now I am picking up the phone every time I see an unidentified number and, unfortunately, that means that I am having to listen to a bunch of political calls. I can't tell you how happy I will be when this election is over. I try to cut the callers off pretty quickly, because I know who I am voting for, and I already have to listen to John talk about his politics enough to raise my blood pressure. There it goes again—

"Hello?"

"Hello, my name is Lorraine. I think you left me a voice-mail about my relatives."

Oh my God!

"Yes! Hello! My name is Jesse Scott. It's so good to talk to you. Thank you so much for calling me back."

OK, I will spare you the details, because we just generally chit chatted for a while. I'm trying to help her get to know me and I end up pouring on the charm, but not so much that she thinks I'm selling her something.

She finally tells me, "You know, the person you really need to talk to is my Aunt Louann. I'm pretty sure Donna is her sister who ran off years ago. Louann lives somewhere in California, but she used to live in Port Orford."

I told her I found some connections to Port Orford in my research already, so that makes a lot of sense. Now I've got a phone number for this Louann woman, and I'm starting to let my hope rise. I have already sent texts to John, Lee, and Rosa with this exciting development. So far, again, Rosa seems to be the only one sharing some of my excitement. I think John is a little worried about me, and Lee is acting like it doesn't matter. I'm sure that Rosa would love it if Lee could find some answers. He's still not talking to my dad, and if I can find our parents, maybe it will help Lee feel like he's gaining a parent.

Sometimes my dad forgets that he and Lee aren't talking, and he calls Lee to see if he'll bring over a bottle of wine or some vodka to his apartment. Apparently, the re-tirement facility where he lives has a van that takes people to the grocery store, but not the liquor store, and if it's late at night and my dad is out of wine, he thinks Lee should be his personal delivery boy. Dad's drinking has gotten heavier as he has gotten older. In some ways you would think that it would be a way for him and Lee to bond. Instead, Lee can see that it's just my dad needing a favor, which doesn't go over well when my dad hasn't been willing to grant Lee any favors recently.

I know Lee really misses our mom. I miss our mom, too. And Sis. I know Sis would be supportive of this journey. Every time I talked to her about it, she would always tell me she would pray for me. Sometimes I felt like that was her way of judging me, but she was a minister, for God's sake. Oops. She probably wouldn't appreciate my using that expression. Sometimes, lately, I find myself telling her about my life. Even though I know she can't actually answer me, I still feel better. Maybe that's how she felt about her prayers.

I wish my sister would have outlived our mom. When my mom was 80, she had to have heart surgery. The anesthesia was pretty hard on her, and we all noticed that her memory was impacted. It turned out to be the early signs of Alzheimer's. I was living in Palm Springs and would come up to Portland for visits, and as the disease progressed, she would sometimes recognize me and sometimes she wouldn't. I would bring her a six-pack of Coke, her favorite, and visit with her. There would be glimpses of recognition that I would try to hold onto.

By the time my mom was moved to her own memory care unit in another facility, she wasn't recognizing many of us most of the time. My dad had to take the bus to see her, so he wasn't able to be with her all the time. To be honest, I think sometimes my dad needed a break. Near the end, my mom slipped into a coma and was placed on hospice. I came up to Portland, and Lee and I took turns sitting with her. Lee was working nights, so I would have the night shift while Lee would stay with her in her room, trying to get some rest for himself. Sometimes my dad or Rosa would be there too.

On my mom's last day, I knew it was happening. I just kept thinking, "Oh my God, this is the end." I held her hand and told her how much I loved her. I told her to not worry about Lee's and Dad's relationship, and I assured her we would all be OK if she wanted to just go ahead and pass. I stroked my mom's hair and told her that she was a great mom. She let out a strange sound as she took her last breath, and then everything was still. I was totally freaking out on the inside, but I was trying really hard to keep it together. I used one hand to call Rosa, not letting go of my mom's hand, as something told me that if I let go and her hand wasn't warm, it would all be real. When Rosa arrived, she took my mom's other hand. I said a prayer, asking God to take my mom into his loving arms. Rosa and I were quietly sitting with her, and even though it was intense, it was also really peaceful and beautiful. I hope I helped her feel safe enough to let go. I hope someone does that for me when it's time.

I called my dad to tell him Mom had passed, and he didn't show much emotion. He let us know he would come over the next morning. Rosa picked out an outfit for Mom to be buried in, and when the funeral home people came to pick her up, I gave her one last kiss on her forehead, which was cold.

The next day my dad took Lee and I out to breakfast. I wish I could say we had a really deep talk about mortality and forgiveness and our lives. We didn't, and that was OK because just being together in peace was what my mom would have wanted for us. We had all been grieving my mom for a while as her illness progressed, and in some ways there was a little relief for my dad.

Things were different, though, when she really did pass. My mom was the parent that showed us affection, and even if she had not been in that role for the last few years, the idea of her was one we had to let go of for good. Sometimes you know in your head that something isn't going to get better, but deep in your heart you keep thinking it might.

Chapter 10

A Sign From God

My life at Merle's house continued on for the rest of the school year. Jimmy and I would lay out by the pool getting a tan, and sometimes we'd walk over to Chief Burgers to get lunch. I remember having our birthday party together. I was turning 15. Roger ended up getting me the album "The Best of Bread," and he wrote a sweet note in my card telling me that he knew I liked to sing. Once in a while I would get glimpses of him being kind. I knew he didn't love that music, so I appreciated the gesture. I'm not sure if the other boys were worried that they would be seen as gay if they were nice to me or if they just really didn't like me. I was getting used to celebrating my birthdays without my parents, but I still wished I could be with Lee, and even though I tried to hide it, I still felt disappointed by their ongoing rejection.

At one point, I was feeling so sick and tired of all of it I just had this feeling of anger move through my body. I was walking home from school and I remember feeling angry at God. How could he let this happen to me ? How could he continue to punish me, even after all the work I had done to pay attention to him. I mean, I grew up going to church and Sunday school, and I did the family devotional stuff, and I even participated in all the religious stuff at St. Mary's. Of course, it seemed like I was just going to church with JoAn to get away from Merle, but I was also trying to talk to God. I know this sounds really corny, but I looked up to the sky and I said, "God, I don't know that I believe in you anymore. I don't know why you are making me feel so miserable. If you do exist, I need a sign. Like, do something to make me believe in you. Make it rain right now or I'm going to stop believing in you forever."

I was crying and my body was shaking, and I'm sure if someone passed me on the street they would think I was crazy. I put my head down and continued to walk home, knowing Merle would be in his room waiting for me. All of a sudden, I felt a drop of water. And then another. It started sprinkling. Now, I know what you're thinking, this was Portland, Oregon in the spring, when it rains all the time and sometimes it happens out of nowhere, even when the sun is out. I didn't care. I felt like this was some sort of sign that things would be OK. It was a sign that God was really there looking out for me on some level I didn't fully understand. In some small way, I felt less alone.

One afternoon, during the summer between sophomore and junior year of high school, I was taking the bus downtown. As I was passing the bus station I looked out the window and saw this kid about my age who was wearing really flamboyant clothing. This was back in the 1970s, and although I had seen hippies around, this felt different. It wasn't the same as hippies, it was more colorful and, well, more feminine. It was as if he was not only gay, but not ashamed of it at all. It was as if he was advertising it.

I happened to be getting off at that stop, and I am trying really hard to remember how we started talking, but it escapes me. I found out that his name was David and he asked if I wanted to walk around with him for a while. He told me he lived downtown in his own apartment and we ended up going there and smoking a little pot. It was really a trip being in a kid's apartment who was my age without any adults. He had these tapestries hanging on the wall and a little stereo in the corner. David figured out I was gay pretty instantly, even though I wasn't wearing the same kind of clothing. He said he got a vibe. I was a little freaked out because that was not the vibe I was trying to advertise, but David made me feel really comfortable, and it was almost as if that gay vibe was what connected us. It was as if my being gay was the thing that was leading to us be friends and not the thing that would get me labeled as crazy or as someone to just be used for sex. It was a little mind blowing to be honest.

I ended up telling David about my situation with Merle.

"Hey man, if this guy is such a horrible old pervert, why don't you just leave?"

He told me that he and his friends were working on the street, and even though they ended up doing some of the same things to these old guys that I was doing to Merle, at least they were making money and living in their own apartments. He even told me I could move in with him until I found my own place, and if I didn't want to do stuff with old guys, maybe I could sell weed or something as a way to make money.

It never occurred to me that I could leave Merle's house or that I had choices. I made the decision right then and there that I wasn't going back. I almost wrote that I wasn't going home, but my home was with Lee and my parents and that wasn't an option anymore. Merle's was just a place I was living. Maybe this could be my new home. I remember thinking to myself, "I guess I'm running away." I took the bus back to Merle's that night with my head swimming thinking of all the possibilities, already figuring out what I would pack and what I would leave behind.

I left Louann a message. I'm getting pretty good at this by now, balancing sounding friendly and upbeat, without coming off as manic or creepy. I'm assuming that Lorraine already called her and gave her a heads up, but I still expect folks to be hesitant. I have no idea how my dad would react if some stranger called trying to get information on his relatives, especially if someone told him my Uncle Jim was their biological dad. I told him with all the money I was spending on Ancestry, I would start to look up his history as well as my mom's. He didn't seem that interested, and he may have made a comment about me looking for my "real mom" that sounded a little indignant. As if by searching, I was intimating that he and my mom weren't enough or something. I sighed but I didn't react, which is why I am still able to talk to my dad.

Lee wouldn't hold back if my dad said something like that to him. Lee still blames my parents for sending him to prison. I mean, Lee did break into their house and steal a bunch of their things, but he thinks my parents shouldn't have turned him in. I guess we both feel like our parents betrayed us in ways that are similar and unique. They both took steps to get rid of us, even if in their eyes we brought it on ourselves. The difference was that I was only thirteen at the time.

I keep thinking about how my dad drove down to San Francisco to scoop me up and bring me home when my meth use was out of control. I don't remind Lee that one time my dad actually drove up to Spokane to help out when Lee had escaped from prison.

It was Christmas morning, and Lee had nothing, and I guess my mom talked my dad into picking him up. That was such a ridiculous situation. Lee was so close to getting out that he was able to have conjugal visits with some woman he met through the mail, and convinced to marry him.

Well, on one of those visits he had this woman help him break out. He says she had stolen a car, and that somehow he hid underneath it when she left the prison. He talks about how they made it to Las Vegas, where they were staying in an apartment complex that her dad managed. The day after they arrived, they were walking back from getting something to eat and saw the parking lot swarming with cops, and somehow they were able to take off without being seen.

Lee tells it with more details, and even talks about how the cops had the wrong room and that the guy who was in that wrong room ended up having a heart attack after they kicked in the door. It sounds like a scene out of a movie. He said there was a SWAT team and it was on the news, which makes it hard for me to understand how he got out of there.

Lee's wife's dad gave them a credit card and they flew to a couple of different places until they split up in Texas. Lee ended up working odd jobs and hitchhiking across the country for the next year. The call to my parents on Christmas happened after Lee was caught in a snowstorm in North Dakota, picked up by a hitchhiker, and dropped off in Spokane. Because it was Christmas, nothing was open, and maybe deep down Lee was actually missing our family.

It's a long drive up to Spokane from Portland, and I can't imagine that was pleasant for either Lee or my dad. But at least my dad didn't call the cops on Lee. Lee says that my dad told him that he didn't want to know anything, and that he had to leave in the morning. He also told him that he didn't want to hear from him again. He gave Lee some money and dropped him off at his wife's best friend's house. Lee ended up getting picked up all on his own about a year later, for something as dumb as driving with a broken tail light, and he headed back to prison for several more years. That woman, the best friend of his wife, ended up pregnant, and that's where Lee's daughter Sabrina came from.

Lee tells me now that he's never going back to jail because he knows that if he does go back, they will basically throw away the key. I feel that way about drugs. I mean, I am not saying I haven't had a little fun once in a while, and I still love a good cocktail. I just know that if I started using meth regularly again, I would lose everything I have worked so hard to build. I definitely wouldn't be able to be a caregiver, and although I assume John would stick around for awhile, he probably wouldn't want to stay forever if I was constantly acting paranoid. Les would still let me live in this house, but who knows how much damage I would inflict. There is actually a hole in the wall from this one time I was paranoid I was being watched by the government. I tore apart the wall to find the wires, and even though that was years ago, I haven't gotten around to fixing it. It's a bit of a reminder about how miserable addiction feels. I don't need to go there again. Lee's been out for so long now that I have learned to relax and trust he'll stick around. I give a lot of credit to Rosa, but Lee deserves a lot of it, too.

Years ago when I worked at Cascade AIDS Project, I had a coworker who was in recovery from a crack cocaine addiction. She carried around an old ID she had when she was using drugs, as a reminder of how far she had come and how much she would lose if she relapsed. When she showed it around, we were all shocked. I didn't need to show my boss an old ID, because I had been a client there who was homeless and using pretty heavily just a year before I was hired. My boss, Dayna, had seen me in that state and she still hired me. She saw something in me that was beyond my worst behavior, and by giving me that job she offered me a chance at redemption. And you know what? I ended up being really good at it. I worked in the transitional housing program with clients who were homeless. I could see right through some of our folks who were not only using drugs. but thought that they could get away with hustling from our agency. A lot of them still tried to rope me back in, telling me I was a sell out, but I stood my ground and tried to come at them with compassion. I tried to see their potential too.

Rosa sees that potential in Lee, and I guess I see my parents the same way too. I can still be angry about them sending me to the hospital and refusing to let me come home. There were times, though, that they were decent to me and maybe that's just the best they could do, even if it wasn't always enough. Now that my mom has passed away, I know that she can't actually say anything to make up for what happened, but I can still try to understand her and come to peace with it. My dad is a little more challenging because he's alive and continues to say hurtful things, but underneath it I know he still loves me in his own way. I just wish he didn't make it so clear how embarrassed he is with the way our lives turned out. Or how disappointed he is that Sis was the child he lost. It's all complicated.

Who knows how I will feel when I do actually find my real mom. Will I feel like she betrayed me too, even if she does end up being Cher? Will this be a chance for her own redemption or for mine?

Chapter 11

Mr. Showmanship

Yesterday I was at work and my phone rang right in the middle of Christopher's shower. I heard it ringing, and tried to stay focused on what I was doing, but something told me that it was a call from Port Orford, Oregon. A call from Louann.

I must say, I remained a complete professional and helped Christopher finish showering, I dried him off, and I helped him get dressed. He was all settled when I checked my voicemail and heard this woman telling me she might have some information for me. I stepped outside and lit a cigarette before calling her back. I know I could have told Christopher what was happening, but for some reason, I wanted to keep it to myself. Having him listening in or even watching me pace around outside would have been too much.

Well guess what? I think I have a new Auntie! Louann was pretty sure the woman I am looking for is actually her sister, Donna. Louann said that she hasn't seen Donna for years. Louann let me know that she heard that Donna had ended up with a Black man, and that didn't go over so well in their family, but Louann let me know that she herself wasn't racist.

I told her that the last name of my father was Martinez, and she said that she thought she heard about that too. Louann alluded to the fact that her sister had left home pretty young after having a difficult life, but that she was much older than Louann, so it wasn't clear why she had taken off. It also sounded like maybe Louann had a different dad, but it was actually hard for me to keep track without writing it all down. It was hard to tell if Louann felt guilty or angry about not knowing what happened to her sister. It mostly sounded like she felt sad about it, and the thought of finding her again sounded pretty great. I didn't ask why she wasn't the one looking for her.

Louann said that she had heard from her brother, Lyle, that Donna had gotten in touch with her Native American side and had been going by the name Donna Bearheart. She told me that might help me find her.

Well, guess what. I found Donna Bearheart on Facebook and she lives in Philadelphia! I immediately sent her a request to add me as a friend but she hasn't replied. Yet. I looked at her page and although most of it is photos of flowers or memes with inspirational quotes, there are indeed some photos of an older woman with people who are biracial. Or Black. I don't know exactly. She doesn't have any photos of herself that I can really look into her face and see myself, but this definitely looks promising.

While Christopher has been supportive, I have two more days here before I drive back to Palm Springs. I figure I can do a little looking while I'm here, as long as I'm handling my duties, but once I get back home I can fully freak out. Maybe the pressure of being here focusing on someone else is actually a good way to keep myself in check.

I know this sounds crazy, but I made plans to meet Louann at her house. Even though her number shows up as Port Orford, she currently lives in a place in the Bay Area that is called Martinez, California. Can you believe it? I told her "Wow! A whole city named after my father!" She kind of chuckled, but I believe it's a sign. Of course, I don't actually believe it was named after the specific Martinez that is my biological father, but what are the odds?

I have asked for time off, and have plans to drive up

there in a few weeks. She told me she would sit down with me and draw out the entire family tree, and this will give her time to dig up some old photos. I guess it's been over fifty years of waiting, so what difference does almost a month make?

Louann told me that the last time she spoke to Donna was twenty years ago when their mother died. Donna told Louann that she had a house in Philadelphia, but didn't share much more information about her life. My sense was that she had been estranged from her sister for so long it was a little like talking about a stranger. Isn't it something that we can do that? We can take some experiences and put them in a little space so that we aren't in so much pain. Do we think that if we do that, time will heal our wounds? I agree that time does take the sting off of grief, but in other situations, it doesn't make that much of a difference. I guess that's how it works with trauma. I know when I first started thinking about my past, it was so overwhelming I would need to smoke a bunch of cigarettes just to help slow down my breathing. Sometimes I would have some weird dreams.

Now that I have been looking back at my life, and hopefully getting ready to meet the very first person who was in my life, it's as if the edges are a little softer. I don't mean it's all fine, it's not. I just don't always feel like it's happening right at this very moment. When I think about those things on my own time, in my own way, it also helps me feel like I have a little more control of the story. Having control over my own story took a long time to gain.

When I finally decided to take control of my life and leave foster care, I didn't end up living downtown with David immediately. I did leave Merle's house and I did start staying with David. Unfortunately, though, I was picked up by the police pretty quickly and charged with a curfew violation and for being a runaway. They called my DHS caseworker, Mr. Green. I told him that he could make me go to another foster home, or another group home, or whatever, but that I would not be going back to Merle's house. He didn't ask and I didn't tell, and I think somehow we both thought it was easier that way.

I'm not saying Mr. Green knew what was going on at Merle's. I'm just saying that DHS caseworkers are overworked and overwhelmed and there probably aren't a lot of foster homes. Having one be accused of sexual abuse would be messy, and I wasn't up for having a bunch of adults accuse me of lying. I also believed that it was only happening to me because I was gay. So I just let it go, and went to a new home. And then another. And then another.

I finally ended up with Cassandra and Philip. They knew that I was gay, and they lived in North Portland in a big house that wasn't that far from Adams High School. They had a baby that I ended up taking care of, and then they took in another foster kid who was younger. I ended up taking care of him too. I also had to clean the house constantly, so if you think about it, it was a pretty good deal for them. They got to collect money from the State of Oregon to have a live-in nanny.

One night while I was in their home, one of their brothers came over. I can't remember if it was Philip or Cassandra's, but it was an adult that I thought of as a foster uncle. Well, he thought it would be fun to start giving me wine and get me drunk. Even though I had been downtown a little, I hadn't really gotten drunk before.

The more wine I drank, the more comfortable I became, and when he started to kiss me and we ended up fooling around, I didn't really care what was happening. Unfortunately, when Philip walked in and found us together, he did care. He started yelling at me and blaming me, even though

I was still just a teenager. I don't remember who said it first, that I should leave, but I do remember telling Philip to "fuck off," and I left the house and headed downtown. David told me I could stay as long as I needed.

A couple of days later, I ended up going to an all-ages club called Second Foundation and I took acid for the first time. Second Foundation was above a leather bar, and a lot of the kids who hung out there were gay. Well, I can tell you the night I took acid was just a kick in the pants. It was such a good trip! I was dancing and there were light trails coming off of everyone. A real body high. I remember feeling so connected and safe, and the next day I called Mr. Green and told him I wanted to be emancipated. I was done letting adults call the shots. They hadn't done a great job of protecting me or supporting me so far, so why not be able to live the way I wanted? Mr. Green couldn't really argue, and he told me he would look into it. I was done waiting on the Scotts to ask me to come home.

John has been trying to be supportive of the recent developments in my search efforts, although when I told him I was planning to visit Louann in person, he may have asked if I was "Fucking Crazy." He keeps saying that this woman is a stranger, but I keep reminding him that I am the one who contacted her out of the blue. If anything, he should be saying that to Louann. How does she know I am not some serial killer or con artist or something?

In the meantime, I have been looking at the property tax rolls in Philadelphia, and I found a home in North Philly that belongs to one Donna Bearheart. There was a phone number attached to it, and of course I called it, but it was disconnected. Even though I had a feeling it would be, my heart was still pounding as I put in the numbers. But still, I have an address. It's on Bosnall Street in North

Philly, and it has her name on it, and this has got to be my mother. I'm thinking about writing a letter. I am also thinking about buying an airplane ticket and hopping on an airplane, and just showing up at the door. Even I think that's fucking crazy, and I don't need John to tell me. Instead, I take a breath and look for my cigarettes.

As I pull out a cigarette, I notice my hand is shaking a little bit. I am trying to figure out why my body is going into freak-out mode. Sure, it's a little scary, but it's also really exciting. What if she has been looking for me the whole time too? I can't stop going over the limited information I have about her, and, unfortunately, part of that is this story about her being a prostitute. What a thing to be defined by, especially by someone who might be your son.

The first time I gave a guy a hand job for money, it was a lot less scary than I expected. I was still so thrilled about not going back to foster care, that it seemed worth it. I know that doesn't make a lot of sense to other people. Was it worse having sex with a whole bunch of different men I wasn't attracted to, or was it worse having sex with one guy who happened to be my foster dad? At least when I was working, it felt like it was my choice. It felt more honest and a lot less incestuous.

I never set out to be a full-time prostitute, but it was what all my new friends were doing. That night I was tripping at Second Foundation, I finally felt free. Well, when I came down and came back to reality, I figured out that feeling free isn't the same as living for free. Turns out that living on your own is expensive, but when you charge between $25 to $150 per trick, you can afford to eat, have clothes to wear, and get a room in an SRO. SRO stands for Single Room Occupancy, and even though they are usually called hotels, they are former hotels that have been turned into cheap housing. Basically, they are the cheapest, most dumpy studio apartments in the downtown area. Most of the buildings have a shared shower down the hall, and the really good ones have a toilet in the room. Most of them have one or two bathrooms on each floor that you share. Some of them have people working at a reception desk downstairs, so it sort of feels like a hotel. Usually that person's job is to either try to keep prostitutes and drugs out of the place, take a cut from the pimps and drug dealers if that is going on there, or call the cops if there is actual violence happening in the lobby. God, I have lived in every SRO in Southwest Portland. We were all just teenagers, trying to figure it out, trying to survive.

We called the area for hustling "Camp." Camp was a space that moved around, rotating between Third, Fourth, and Fifth Streets between Southwest Yamhill and Southwest Salmon streets in downtown Portland. While Stark Street ended up being where all the gay bars were located, Camp was where the prostitution happened. At least if you wanted a boy.

Back in the late 1970s, Portland was a much more industrial and dingy place than it is now. We didn't have coffee shops and condos on every corner, or all the fancy stuff the rich Californians eventually brought to the city. All the older homeless folks hung out on Burnside Street in the Skid Row district. There were some women working over there, and that was still the street to score hard drugs. The gay boys were over in Southwest though, as if we were different.

The men, our customers, would drive by and pull along the street real slow, looking out their windows as we stood around smoking cigarettes, trying to look cute. I'm not sure how it is with Johns who are looking to sleep with women, but with these guys there was that added layer of homophobia going on with them, and you could just sense their self loathing and disgust coming right out the windows. I even felt sorry for some of them. In some ways, it was easier to focus on their self loathing than on our own. Pity them instead of ourselves.

Once in a while, you would get a rich guy who came through and he would want you for a whole weekend. You could make $500 and spend the time in his hotel room, or even his house, if his wife was away. It wasn't always straightforward sex like you would think. These guys would be into all sorts of weird stuff. Some days my elbow got more action than the rest of me. I try to laugh about it, but I don't romanticize it.

I'm sure David and the rest of the guys who were out there are dead by now. I wondered about my biological mom, and if this was what it was like for her if she was a prostitute. I wondered if that was why she had me and Lee so close together. I can't imagine she would make much money if she was knocked up, although maybe there's a market for that kind of thing. I wondered if she hated herself as much as I did. At least I didn't need to worry about getting pregnant.

I was also supplementing my income at the time by selling weed. Not large quantities or anything, just little dime bags to my friends or to Johns who were interested. During this time I wasn't having any contact with the Scotts. Lee was starting to get in trouble too, running away and stealing stuff. There was one time that Lee and his friends came downtown in a stolen car and picked me up to go joy riding. I think he ended up getting arrested for that one, and somehow he blamed me for telling the cops about it.

Thinking back to my time at Camp, there were so many crazy stories. When I was 18 or 19, I met this guy, Mark, who worked in the entertainment industry. He was in his

30s, and he really preferred the younger boys. We only had sex once, but he would end up coming around in his limousine to see if we wanted to party. One weekend he offered to take me to Los Angeles with him. Of course, I thought that was a great idea! I was always up for a break from the rain, and I think on his end I was someone he could be seen in public with, rather than an underage kid.

He took me to brunch at a restaurant in West Hollywood that was upscale, but not too over-the-top fancy. Well, who walks in, but Liberace himself. I was starstruck! Mark noticed I kept looking over and he asked if I wanted to go meet him. Mark walked over and talked to him, and then motioned me to join him.

I was so nervous.

"Hello, Mr. Liberace."

"Oh Honey, don't call me Liberace! Call me Lee!"

He was so welcoming and friendly, as he asked us to join his table. He ordered champagne for the table and just continued to tell jokes with that voice. I wanted to pinch myself.

We flew back home Sunday night and switched out cars. Mark urged me to ask around at Camp to see if a couple of the younger guys wanted to go to the little town of Astoria, on the Oregon Coast for the night. He offered to get us a hotel room.

Astoria is a couple of hours away from Portland, and when we arrived, it was already getting late. Mark had been quiet, but I assumed he was tired from his trip, or maybe just lost in his thoughts. He turned to me before getting out of the car and told me that his chest had been hurting, and that he just didn't feel right. He wondered if maybe we should drive back to Portland and go to the Emergency Room.

I told Mark to trade places, and I drove back to Portland as quickly as I could, making it back in record time. I took Mark to Providence Hospital, and took the boys back to Camp. Mark thanked me and reached into his wallet and pulled out some money. I told him I would return with his car and check on him the next day. He agreed, and even though this guy just gave me his car, I was true to my word and returned the next day.

I passed an older man and a woman in her thirties in the hallway that turned out to be Mark's father and sister. Mark let them know that his friend Jesse would be coming by, and obviously I didn't clarify our relationship. I did, actually, consider Mark a friend. Mark told me that he had experienced a cardiac event, and that the staff at the hospital told him that if he wouldn't have come in, there was a chance that he would have died. In a hotel room in Astoria with three young sex workers. We looked at each other and smiled, feeling lucky to have avoided such a scandal. That would have been messy for all of us.

I was in my apartment five or six days later, when I received a call from Providence Hospital. They told me that Mark had given them my number, and they regretted having to tell me that Mark had died. My heart sank and I started to shake all over. I can't remember how I found out about the funeral, but I showed up with a couple of my friends to pay our respects. Even though Mark was technically a trick, he did treat us pretty well, and we did care for him. We were standing there awkwardly when his mother spotted us and came over. I thought that she was going to thank me for saving her son's life, and I held out my hand to introduce myself. Before I knew what was happening, she hauled off and smacked me across the face and started yelling at me.

"How dare you show up here?! You Dirty Homosexuals!"

Mark's father remembered meeting me at the hospital.

He took my arm and led me away while someone comforted his wife. He told me it was probably a good idea that I leave.

Liberace wasn't the only celebrity I was able to meet. When I was in my early twenties I moved down to Los Angeles. I did do a little modeling, but the truth was that I was back out hustling, spending a lot of time "hitchhiking" on Santa Monica Boulevard. There was a middle aged man who picked me up and took me to his house. He told me he was married to an actress that I vaguely knew but I won't name here. There were huge portraits of this "Unnamed Starlet" in their lovely home, and we spent the afternoon together. Apparently she was off shooting a movie, or was in a production on Broadway. He didn't seem concerned that she would find out. In fact, he asked if I would like to accompany him to a live taping of a show the next day. It was a tribute show to Mr. Television himself, Milton Berle. Of course I wanted to go.

When we arrived at the studio for the event, there were seats that were reserved for us. On one of the seats said his name, and on my seat it said, "Unnamed Starlet's Nephew." I smiled. I was happy to pretend to be her nephew if it meant I was able to stay and enjoy the show.

The show was wonderful, with all of the old vaudeville stars coming to participate. We were able to go backstage afterwards and there were celebrities everywhere. Out of the corner of my eye I spotted Lucille Ball. That was when I really started to freak out. I loved "I Love Lucy" growing up, and here she was, sitting in a chair with a cigarette in a long holder in one hand, and a drink in the other hand. My date noticed my excitement and asked if I wanted to go meet her.

As we approached, my date talked to Ms. Ball with clear familiarity. He introduced me as his wife's nephew. Well,

Lucile Ball looked me up and down and then took a drag off her cigarette. She let out a laugh and rolled her eyes and said, "Nephew, huh? HA!" I recently looked up the "Unknown Starlet" and Wikipedia says that she was one of the first celebrities to come out in support of people living with HIV. I wonder if she and her husband had some kind of arrangement. Maybe she had her own "husband's niece" that she took to events. I hope so.

There is one story that I still giggle about every time I think of it. It was another story from my time in Los Angeles. I remember it was already mid afternoon, and I was still recovering from the previous night. I was partying pretty heavily at the time, and I had already blown my rent money on speed. I was out on the street waiting for something to happen. Daytime tricks were always unpredictable.

A large black limousine pulled up, and I looked around to see if it was meant for someone else. The passenger window rolled down, and the driver motioned for me to come closer. The driver explained that I was invited to join "a party" at his employer's house. I would be given $200, but only on the condition that I would not laugh while at the party. The driver explained there would be other young men, and we would be given food and drinks. If I did laugh, though, I would immediately be asked to leave and would not get paid.

I was all-in. A limo. A rich client. Free food and drinks. Plus, I wouldn't be the only one there, which was always a bonus for safety reasons. I opened the back door and joined several other young men who were in the back of the limo. All of them had drinks and I quickly had one in my hand, too. We were all trying to figure out where we were going and who this mystery employer was that had such weird instructions.

The limo drove for several miles until it wound its way

up the hills of Laurel Canyon. The car pulled into a large home, and we all looked at each other and shrugged. None of us knew this place, even the ones who routinely visited rich guys in this neighborhood.

We were led into a large room where there was a bartender and trays of food. We started helping ourselves, and were encouraged by the staff. The driver reminded the group about the conditions of their payment, that if anyone laughed they would be sent home without pay. Again, we all shrugged and drank and ate, forgetting for a moment that at some point we would be expected to do something to earn this money.

A set of pocket doors in the back of the room opened to reveal another large room with an oversized marble staircase. At the top of the stairs, a nude man was crouched on all fours. We were ushered into the room by the driver. A hush fell over the room.

I had partied with many older men. In fact, they was the majority of my clientele. This guy, though, was ancient. Wrinkly and translucent white, continuing to be crouched down. The older man started licking his hands, as if they were paws, and slowly began to make his way down the stairs. As he turned to the side, the group saw that a large feather duster was inserted into his anus, so that the handle was barely visible and the feathers appeared as if he had a tail. The man took his time crawling down the stairs, purring from time to time, and shaking his behind so that his tail would move about.

My eyes widened and I started to giggle before remembering to stifle it. Now I understood, and the need for $200 was enough to keep it down. Watching this hairless, wrinkled "cat" sidle up to the legs of other young men was both fascinating and excruciating. I bit the inside of my lips as the giggle tried to escape.

The old "cat" turned toward me and crawled over. He nuzzled my leg, rubbing his face on my shin. I wasn't sure if I was supposed to "pet" his head, or just keep still. The driver, who had joined the group, approached me and whispered in my ear,

"Don't you want to pet the pretty pussy?"

My laugh exploded out of my body. Everything came out and I found myself doubled over, tears spilling from my eyes as the absurdity of the situation, of my life, just poured out. Several other men lost it as well. It was as if a dam burst and the ripple effect was infectious. The sound of whooping and snorting and laughing filled the quiet room. The driver tapped me on the shoulder and pointed at the door. The other laughing men followed suit. We piled back into the limo, giggling and still doubled over.

As the laughter died down, the men looked at each other and then turned toward me.

"Damn, Bitch! You just cost me two hundred dollars!"

I held up my hands, "I'm sorry! Believe me, I need this money too!"

They all tried to look stern and pissed, but waves of giggles would erupt and we would all start in again. I leaned back into the seat and wiped my eyes and thought about where I might try to make some money later that night. Even though I blew it, I also knew this would make one hell of a great story one day.

I don't mean to glamorize this part of my life. Yes, there were brushes with celebrities, and wild stories, but there was a really dark side to it too. I only had a gun pulled on me once, which in some warped way is considered lucky. I was back in Portland and was picked up by a guy in a VW Bug. He told me he wanted a blow job but he didn't have anywhere private to go.

I said, "I'm fine to just lean over and do it in the car if

you want to unzip your pants."

"No. No way. I can't have anyone seeing this. See that car over there? I think they might be watching us. Let's drive somewhere."

He started driving and he kept looking around and saying things that just seemed paranoid.

"What about that car? Have you seen that car before? Do you think they could be following us?"

The next thing I knew, we were on I-5, headed to Washington State. He finally pulled over, and I was just wanting to get this over with so I could get paid and get back to downtown Portland. He pulled over in some empty parking lot and I looked out the passenger window, trying to see if anyone else was around. When I turned around I saw the barrel of a gun pointing at me. He called me a faggot.

I don't know what came over me, and I will be the first to admit that this was really stupid, but I just spit in his face and screamed at him:

"Take me back to fucking Portland you psycho! Now! Start driving!"

I was so angry I was shaking. Well, damned if he didn't start driving. He kept the gun pointed at me but at least we were heading in the right direction. At one stop light I tried to unlock the door. He saw me and put the gun right against my head. I couldn't believe that after all I had gone through, this was how I was going to die. I started praying to God.

By the time we got back downtown, this guy drove me back to where we could see the rest of the boys standing around waiting for tricks. He told me to send a couple of other boys his way. I agreed and tried to hide my shaking hands. I forced myself to walk slowly and naturally back to the group, and I kept my voice low as I told the other guys he had a gun. A few of us started to walk toward his car, but then suddenly bolted into a nearby restaurant. He gunned his engine and took off.

We sat in that coffee shop for a while, making sure he didn't return. I was pretty upset and the other guys surrounded me with love while I cried and shook. We felt so helpless. It's not like we could call the cops or anything. Even though I still really needed some money, I couldn't bring myself to do any more work that night. Instead, I went to a gay disco and danced and let men buy me drinks until 2:30 a.m. I was back out at Camp the next night.

My parents knew that I was out there doing this for work, and even though they obviously didn't approve, I think they also realized that they had not given me much choice. There was a fellow congregant at their church, Edith Green, who had been a U.S. Congresswoman. She was a pretty big deal. I guess she had announced that she wanted to start a project to support street kids and sex workers in Portland, and my parents actually told her about my situation and helped us connect.

I met Ms. Green at the République Café twice, and I told her all about what it was like to be living on the streets and working in the sex trade. She was very respectful and took a lot of notes while we talked. I told her that most of us were estranged from our families, and she didn't defend my parents or even really acknowledge them. Even though she seemed more interested in the experience that young women were having, she did thank me and she even mentioned that she would like me to be on an advisory committee for a shelter she was planning to open.

The Green House Shelter did end up opening in a space that was a former gay bar, the Family Zoo, and it was run by the Salvation Army. She never actually asked me to be on her advisory committee. That's OK. I felt so important having had those conversations with her about my life, I could forgive her for not following through on that idea. I knew she was a really important person, and she made me feel like my experiences were not only valid, but that sharing them with her would help her to provide support to other people like me.

I told my closest friends about the experience, but overall I tried to keep it private. Even though I felt like it was a really positive, constructive experience, I knew that the other guys would call me a narc or a sellout. I cared enough about my reputation to keep my mouth shut, but I also knew this was a positive thing. That feeling of doing something positive to help my community, at the risk of my street cred, would come up again later in my life when I got a job at Cascade AIDS Project. I get it. It's hard to know who to trust sometimes when you are in that life. it feels like everyone else who isn't is trying to get in your way, or is somehow contributing to your exploitation. They did end up naming a federal building after Edith Green in Portland, so she was in fact a pretty big deal.*

I'm off work and back in Palm Springs now, so I can fully devote myself to this Ancestry project. I keep looking at this Facebook page for Donna Bearheart. She won't accept my friendship as Jesse Scott, but what if I create a new page under the name of Jesus Martinez? I mean, she wouldn't know Jesse Scott, and obviously she wouldn't recognize me in my photo. I'm guessing I look a little different now that I'm 59 years old and not a toddler. She is probably thinking Jesse Scott is just a robot or something. Rosa said that she would send her a friend request too. Oh wait, there's my phone with Rosa texting now.

"Jesse! Donna Bearheart just accepted my friend request!"

Holy smokes! I immediately text Rosa back, and I wonder why she accepted her request and not mine and I try to stop myself from having some feelings about it. I'm sure it has something to do with Rosa looking sweet and non-threatening. Who knows why people do what they do? It's still pretty thrilling, and I wonder if Donna is figuring it out. I'm still going to create this other Facebook profile. Here's another text from Rosa:

"Holy shit. She just unfriended me. But now she has a bunch of my memes on her page. What the hell?"

Well I guess I don't need to be jealous after all. I'm sending this friend request as Jesus Martinez, but I'm still using my same profile photo because I do look pretty handsome in it. I text Rosa to see if I should do it, and this is her reply:

"God dammit, Jesse. Just do it. Just hit send!"

And so I do.

Chapter 12

Finding Family

The first thing I noticed when I drove into Martinez, California was the smell of oil in the air. Louann had warned me that it was a city built around a refinery and that the smell can be a little overwhelming. She let me know she didn't notice it anymore, which is what happens when you're in a place long enough. I wish that was the case with the heat in Palm Springs.

Louann's house was small but nice. I was nervous as I rang the bell, but after driving for seven hours, I was also pretty tired and glad to get out of the car. My nerves started to melt away when she opened the door and gave me a big hug. Louann was so warm and welcoming, and she introduced me to her husband, Vaughn as "my long lost nephew." I ended up staying four days. Even though I was in a hotel, I spent most of my time at her home.

Louann had chickens and roosters in the backyard, along with rabbits, cats, and a pond with Koi fish. Vaughn wasn't doing too well. He had a pretty serious case of emphysema and mesothelioma and was on oxygen. He would go to bed each night around 7 p.m. and Louann and I would stay up all night and look at pictures, telling each other our stories.

Louann was almost as curious about Donna as I was, and she explained that Donna had left home at age 15. Louann was only four years old when she left, and no one had heard from her for 40 years. Louann said that Donna had actually called the family home after having a premonition that her mother had died. When she called her mom to make sure she was alive, Louann's sister answered the phone and let Donna know that their mother had indeed passed. Donna told them she was living in Philadelphia, but didn't share many other details about her life. That was the last time anyone heard from her.

I told Louann I was gay when we talked on the phone. She let me know that she didn't mind, and she asked a lot about John, which was pretty different from my own parents, who liked to pretend as though John didn't exist. Louann is a member of the Yurok tribe of Northern California and is really in touch with that part of her heritage. I have to say, those nights we stayed up late were the first time I felt like I could look into someone else's face and actually feel like I could relate to them. Like somehow we belonged to each other on a deeper level. Like I wasn't just dropped into some family out of nowhere.

Louann told me stories about her family, which I guess also means Donna's family, which I suppose means my family. She told me that Donna's mother was Nellie and that she was Native American. She said that Donna's brother Lyle was a year younger than Donna and that her sister Glenna was two years younger. Their dad's name was James, and at some point, the three kids went to live with their aunt Maude. She wasn't sure why, but she thinks that somehow it's tied in to the reason why Donna left at such a young age.

I end up writing all of them down to list them out:

Hoopa Sally.

Adelia, born 1859.

Nellie, born March 10, 1903, married to James Hurst.

Nellie and James have a baby, Glenn, who dies of SIDS (So sad.)

She then had Joe, Gloria, Donna, Lyle, and Glenna.

Nellie leaves James Hurst and is with someone

named Johnson, has another baby named Sonny, but everyone knows James Hurst is the father (So scandalous, I love it!)

James remarries and has three more kids – Sam, Delores, and Helen.

Nellie has Louann.

No wonder Louann lost touch with Donna. From what I can figure out, Nellie had eight kids. I try to track the dates, but end up getting confused and instead I just listen to the stories, which Louann tells me is the Native way. She tells me that Hoopa Sally was "famous." Apparently she and her brother Billy had something to do with some land rights or something pretty confusing, but hey, I will take a famous relative any day.

Louann tells me about Sally's daughter, Adelia. Apparently when Adelia was a young woman, she was out on her boat, fishing off the reservation. She was followed, and then raped by a member of the Calvary. Legend has it, she pulled out her bowie knife and stabbed him in self defense. Gutted him, actually. I assume this happened while the assault was happening or immediately after the fact, when he had his pants down. She paddled back to the reservation and was never able to leave, as she knew that once she left the protection of her home she would be hanged for murdering a white man.

Of course my eyes are huge and I'm squealing, and Louann is giggling at my reaction, and we both need to keep it down so Vaugh doesn't wake up. My head is reeling and I keep thinking that in all my years with the Scotts, I have never heard stories this dramatic. Even though I am hearing about strangers, I feel like I know these women, or if not the women, I know their struggle. For the first time, this knowing actually feels like power rather than just like shame. I know what it's like to be terrified and to somehow dig deep and find the power to survive. Louann doesn't smoke, but she hangs out with me outside while I pull out an American Spirit.

Apparently, Hoopa Sally was 100% Native American, but when she had Adelia it was with a white man, so Adelia was ½ Native. Her daughter, Nellie, was ¼ Native. Donna and Louann are ⅛ Native, which would make me ¹⁄₁₆th. Louann is a member of the Yurok tribe and I try to follow how the Hoopa and Yurok tribes were feuding over the years, which involved some property disputes and a long standing lawsuit about money. It sounds like even though Louann's grandmother was Hoopa, her mother—Nellie's last husband—was in the Yurok tribe, and he left his estate to Nellie and her descendants. All those years my dad tried to include us in these lessons about Native Americans just felt so generic, as if all the tribes were the same. Talking to Louann, who is very connected to this part of her story, brings it to life in a way that feels completely different.

I left Martinez and drove north to Crescent City to meet Louann's siblings, Joe and Gloria. Joe was a little gruff and we really only spent an hour together. He showed me some of the crafts he made, including arrowheads. I later heard what Joe told my cousin, Rita, after he met me, "He has a ponytail and he looks white!"

Gloria met with me for four or five hours and was pretty friendly. She wasn't doing too well with her health so I didn't push it.

I spent a few days with some of their kids, which I guess would be my cousins, which still sounds so strange to say out loud. There was Melissa, Cheryl, and Rita. They all asked to see my birth certificate, but were otherwise pretty open. We mostly went to bars, and it didn't hurt that I was buying the drinks. I hope that doesn't come off as mean. I don't want to sound like I thought they were judging me or using me for my money; they weren't. They were actually quite open. They took me to the Yurok tribal offices to introduce me and helped me get the paperwork to fill out to be a member. That seemed like a long shot, but again, their offer to introduce me was pretty special. As if I was literally being offered membership into a tribe. I kept hearing John's voice in my head, "Do what you need to do Jesse, but please be careful." I'm sure he wouldn't like that I was buying drinks and dinner for everyone, but none of them asked for it. It seemed like they didn't have a lot of money, and if they thought I was there to rip them off somehow, I wanted to ease their minds. They all gave me hugs and wished me luck and told me to not be a stranger. My head was swimming as I drove back to Palm Springs.

I'm struck by this family's ability to trust me. I know that at my age and with what I am doing in my life, I deserve to be trusted. I am trustworthy. That definitely wasn't the case though when I was hustling. I'm not saying I would rip off tricks. It was just that I started using so many drugs that I made some really stupid decisions and many times that involved hurting people.

I'm not trying to use this as an excuse, but when your main source of income involves having sex with strangers, using drugs is a really tempting way to get through it. I used pretty much anything I could get my hands on, but methamphetamine was my favorite and it was everywhere. When I look back on my life, it is painful to think about all the times I was a victim. It is a different feeling to think about ways that I was a victimizer. Shame feels different in your body.

For a short time, it looked like I would be able to get out of the street life. I was working at the Coliseum Holiday Inn and even though I was still using drugs, I was able to show up to work and be charming. I had a friend, Rianne, who worked with me. We were using this new business software at the hotel, and the two of us worked up a plan to start a business of our own. We would be training companies to use this system, as it was going into all sorts of businesses. We called ourselves "Hands On Training" and for a little while we were having some success.

Even though I was still dabbling in drugs, it took a lot of effort to run a business, and I needed to have my head on straight at least some of the time. We were both offered positions working for a company called Action Software in San Diego, with a salary of $35k a year, which in 1984 was pretty great. Rianne didn't want to move, but I jumped at the chance. I had picked up some accounting skills, and so all of the sudden I found myself with a real job in a new town. I felt like it was a chance to have a fresh start.

Unfortunately, my fresh start didn't come with any new type of coping skills, and I immediately found the drug dealers down in San Diego. It's not like it was that difficult, as most of the gay bars were filled with them, I tried to keep my job, but it's hard to go to work consistently when you are on a multi day binge and you show up to work tweaking. I remember one time I was in my office with a loaded syringe, about to shoot up, when a coworker walked in. I sternly scolded them for interrupting me while I was taking my insulin. Can you believe my nerve? Well, my boss didn't believe that I was injecting insulin, and I was eventually fired. Instead of seeing it was time to get clean, I just ramped up how much I was using.

After I lost my job, I would spend my days walking around the city, usually tweaking. I was out one day when all of the sudden I felt a really intense pain in my side and my legs gave out as I doubled over. I was writhing around on the sidewalk when some nice stranger called an ambulance. I was taken to the hospital and admitted for pneumonia. I remember the look on the doctor's face when, the next day, he came into my room to tell me I had tested positive for this new disease called ARC, which stood for AIDS Related Complex.

AIDS had been around for six or seven years at that point, and of course I had heard of it, as a bunch of the people I knew were dropping like flies. It's weird, though, to think about now. ARC isn't even a diagnosis anymore and I remember feeling sad, as well as numb, but completely not surprised.

I wish I could say that it changed my perspective on life. To be honest, it just felt like it was one more shitty thing that happened to me, or that somehow I had brought it on myself.

I ended up staying in the hospital for four weeks, which seemed like a year, focusing on getting my lungs back. They didn't offer me any medicine for AIDS, because there wasn't really anything back then. I know it's cool to be a trendsetter, but take it from me, when it comes to chronic diseases you should really try to get one that has been around awhile.

I went home and within no time I was using again, trying to ignore this new recent diagnosis. I know most people with a serious disease that compromises your immune system would want to do everything in their power to eat healthy and try to avoid getting sick. The brain of a drug addict doesn't work that way though, at least not my brain.

One day, my boyfriend decided to take my car with some friends, and they ended up stealing another car. There was a checkbook and ID in the car, and in my drug-addled brain, I thought that it would be a good idea to start writing checks on this poor guy's account. We figured out that he was a veterinarian, and we just assumed he had plenty of money. I started off going to stores and buying stuff like blenders, small appliances, nice clothes. I would write a check for my purchases and then return them later for cash. Well, that was working out pretty well and I was making enough to pay my basic bills and buy more drugs. Then I got greedy.

I remember being at the car lot, totally tweaking, and letting the sales people know I was interested in buying a Camaro Z28. It was THE car of that era. They let me test drive it and agreed that I would come back the next day to finish all the paperwork before handing over the keys.

Again, this sounds really embarrassing and dumb and of course it wasn't going to go well, but back then the drugs were the ones making all these dumb decisions. When I returned the next day, I signed all the paperwork and then one of the guys at the car dealership flashed a badge, and I was immediately arrested. I was charged with "Attempted Grand Theft Auto," "Forgery," "Fraud," and they also charged me with "Grand Theft Auto" for the original car theft. I admitted to the first string of charges, but I was adamant about the fact that I wasn't the one to steal the car in the first place.

I was devastated. I was filled with shame. I was terrified. I had a public defender, and somehow they were able to persuade the judge to drop that last charge and to give me one year minus a day in jail. If you are sentenced to over a year, you go to prison, but if it is less than a year you stay in County jail, which seems like a much less scary option.

In some ways, being in jail reminded me of being in the mental hospital, except that in jail all of the people were dangerous. The first night I was there, I was coming down from meth and sleeping on the floor in a big open room filled with other prisoners. I was waiting to be assigned to my own cell. Someone jumped on me and punched me in the eye while I was trying to sleep. I didn't see who did it, and in the morning when the guards asked me why I had a black eye, I told them that I tripped and fell into something.

It was the right move. I wasn't seen as a snitch, and somehow that helped me gain some respect. I was obviously really outwardly gay, and I had all these fears about "dropping the soap" in the shower, but none of that ever happened. My cellmate was actually gay too, and we ended up getting in a fight. I can't even remember what it was about, but it escalated pretty quickly, and before I knew what was happening, it was like a scene out of a movie where everyone made a ring around us and they were all cheering us on.

I had never hit anyone beyond wrestling with Lee, and I ended up giving this guy a shiner and gaining even more respect from the other prisoners. I felt bad about it and later in our cell I apologized. My apology didn't make it less awkward to share a space that small.

Beyond getting in that fight, I was actually a model prisoner. I did all my chores without complaining, and I ended up getting along with everyone. Again, I felt like my training at Dammasch set me up to be pretty used to that institutional structure. I didn't use drugs when I was there and after 6 months they let me go with something called a "Mid Term Modification." I was given three years probation and I begged them to send me back to Portland. All of my friends in San Diego were using drugs, and I felt like I had a better shot at staying clean if I was back in Oregon. I wish I could say my plan worked. I did indeed return to Oregon but I was using before I even made it to the bus station.

Once I returned to Oregon, I got hooked up with a doctor and a place to live and various social services for people with HIV. I started taking AZT, which in those days was taken by the handful. That was when it really hit me. I told Lee that I was HIV positive, and for once he didn't tease me about being gay. My parents didn't take the news well, but at that point I think they were just so disgusted by the drugs and jail that they weren't that surprised, either.

I was living in an apartment at a big public housing building called Hollywood East. It was set in the Hollywood neighborhood in Portland, which, believe me, is a far cry from Hollywood, California. It was a huge building that originally housed seniors, but at some point was also opened up to younger people with disabilities. The two populations did not mix well at all.

I'm sure the seniors were scared of me, because the drugs were making me pretty psychotic most of the time. I was experiencing auditory hallucinations, delusions, and a lot of paranoia. I have no idea why I would keep doing that to myself, but even though there were times that were miserable, meth also gave me a blast of euphoria I felt like I desperately needed. I just wish it wasn't so complicated.

One night I called Lee and begged him to come over. I was convinced there were people outside my window. My window on the 14th floor. Lee came over with his dog and when he walked in I grabbed his arm and told him that "Mom and Dad are in the bathroom!"

Lee looked in the bathroom and said, "Hey Jesse. I don't see Mom and Dad there. I think you're just tweaking."

"No, no, no, no, no. Listen, Lee. They're in there. They're just hiding. I know you think I'm tweaking, but I saw them. I saw someone outside the window too. They keep harassing me. You gotta believe me. They were here just a minute ago and now they're just hiding." Meanwhile, my jaw was moving a mile a minute.

Lee somehow convinced me that our parents were not in the bathroom, there was not anyone outside my window, and that the neighbors were most likely not listening to me. In fact, the neighbors probably wanted me to shut the hell up. Lee was actually pretty patient with me while I was one tweaky little mess. Lee was using meth in those days, too, but he was using it with his motorcycle gang and I don't know how to explain it, but it had a very different flavor to it.

I was spending my days at the HIV Day Center and was probably the messiest I ever made myself. What's sad is that it was all self made. I know now that trauma plays a huge role in addiction, and I'm not sure if I was trying to slowly kill myself, or I just didn't think I deserved anything better. It was like all the awful, shitty stuff in my life was coming to a head, and I was drowning in it. I had lost a lot of weight and I looked like hell, and I kept this up for years. I was finally evicted from Hollywood East for not paying my rent, and I was back living in SROs.

One day I saw a flier at the HIV Day Center that was looking for volunteers to serve on the Ryan White Care Council to help decide how to distribute money for HIV services. I figured I had a lot of opinions about how things should be done, and maybe they needed to hear from people who were actually using those services.

I served for one year, and even though I was still tweaking, I wouldn't use anything before going to one of those meetings. I also started being a client advocate at the Day Center, and then I joined the Board of Directors for the Partnership Project, which was a program that was providing case management to people living with HIV.

At this point, I was having to plan my tweaks and the more I filled up my time with positive things to do, the less time I had to use drugs. I had tried to go Narcotics Anonymous in the past and it didn't really work for me. I know the 12 steps have helped millions of people get clean over the years, and I want to be clear that I totally support those programs. It just didn't work for me.

I had even gone to a short 28 day inpatient treatment program when I was still at Hollywood East, and clearly that didn't work either. What worked was focusing on trying to be helpful and being around people that weren't also in the thick of using drugs.

Sometime in the mid 1990s, Cascade AIDS Project, which was an AIDS organization in Portland, posted a job announcement for a Transitional Housing Specialist. I had been a client of CAP for years, and was living in an apartment through an organization called Ecumenical Ministries. I had a roommate and we were able to get along OK. I was more stable than I had been in years, although that didn't mean I was clean and sober.

I applied for the job and was turned down. Well, I called someone who worked there and I made a big stink about how "CAP likes to talk the talk of serving people with HIV, but when it came time to walk the walk they were just a bunch of hypocrites." I laid it on pretty thick, and may have even said that I wondered how folks at the Ryan White Council would feel about this decision. I know, I know, the nerve!

The next day I got a call from a woman named Dayna and she offered me the position. Dayna had seen me as a client, and said that she could see that I had potential and she wanted to give me a chance to shine. I couldn't believe it. I knew that my drug days needed to end. This was a full time paid position helping people with HIV get into housing. I was finally ready to get my shit together, and I was almost 40 years old.

Driving back to Palm Springs, these memories are just flooding my system. What if Louann and my new cousins find out about this part of my life and realize I was a horrible druggie who had actually been in jail? Would I still be welcomed into their tribe? I know on some level we all have parts of our past we want to hide. We have those parts that come from our deepest brokenness. When I started working at CAP, so many of my fellow addicts saw me as a sellout, just how I feared my friends would see me when I talked to Edith Green all those years ago. I know that their anger was coming from a place of envy, or, even deeper, from a place of fear. Maybe it was a fear that success and change would never be an option for them. Or maybe it was the fear that they would be forced to change their own ways, or would be judged. Maybe it was just a challenge to their status quo and their understanding of who was on one side and who was on the other.

Maybe someday I can actually share my whole story with my new family members and maybe they won't reject me. Obviously, I am not going to tell them everything the first time I meet them. I don't think that is the same as lying. I think we all need time to get to know each other and to build trust. Unconditional love doesn't happen just because you see a name on a birth certificate.

When I find my biological mother she will be faced with the knowledge that I know she gave me and Lee away. She won't be able to hide that part of her past. Will I be able to extend the same empathy and understanding and acceptance to her that I want from my new aunt and cousins? I light a cigarette and turn up the radio as I drive toward the desert.

Chapter 13

Jesus Martinez

It's midnight in Palm Springs and Donna Bearheart just accepted a friend request from Jesus Martinez. I'm freaking out so hard right now. I wonder what she's thinking? I only have one photo, and really basic information on this page, so I am curious to know who she thinks I am. If anything, this new fake profile looks more like a robot than my real page. I mean, poor Jesus Martinez doesn't even have any other Facebook friends.

Here's a message on Facebook Messenger from Donna Bearheart!

"I'm not sure who you are, but something is telling me to accept this friend request."

Oh my God oh my God oh my God. I take a breath and type back–

"I know this may be a lot to hear or to believe, but my name is Jesse Scott. I was adopted and my birth name was Jesus Martinez. I have reason to believe that you are my birth mother. If you want to give me a call to talk, here is my number."

I hesitate and then I hear Rosa's voice in my head to "just do it, dammit," and so I hit send. I'm tempted to wake John up, but I need to not let him talk me out of any of this.

And now my phone is ringing.

Oh my GOD! What should I do? It's a Pennsylvania number and my phone is ringing and I know it's my birth mom and what do I do? I'm shaking so hard right now I can hardly breathe, but if I don't answer it I might never have this chance again. It has rung twice. Now three times. I think I have five rings before it goes to voicemail. I can't do this. But I have to do this. It's been my whole life. Now four rings.

"Hello?"

"Is this Jesus? This is Donna Bearheart. I think I might be your mom."

"Yes! This is Jesus, although I go by Jesse now. I think I might be your son!"

"Are you there with Pete?"

"Who's Pete?!"

Fuck it, I'm smoking in the house! That is, if my hand will stop shaking long enough to use the lighter.

Apparently Pete was the first child Donna had that she put up for adoption. He was born a year before me. I tell her that I'm not with Pete, but I am with Lee, who is known to my mother as José. She is referring to him as "Joe" and she tells me she's been looking for us her whole life. Jesse, Joe and Pete. It's not our birth order, but I guess it just flows better that way. It's so bizarre. As I am having this conversation with this woman, I find myself almost dissociating a little bit. I keep thinking to myself, I did it. I found my mother! We end up talking for over an hour.

One of the first things I say to my birth Mom, this woman Donna, is this:

"Now listen, I need you to know something up front. I'm gay. I have always known I'm gay, and I need you to know this and to know I'm not going to change."

"Oh son, I don't care about that at all. I have some grandkids that go that way and I don't have any judgments about that. But listen, I have something that I need you to know right up front too. I'm with the Blacks now. I have seven other kids besides you, and Pete and Joe, and all of them were with Black men. I hope you don't have a problem with that because I don't mess with white people anymore."

I burst out laughing.

"Donna, first of all, I don't have any judgments about that at all. But did you think I didn't know that? Your whole Facebook page is filled with pictures of Black people! That's totally fine with me!"

Donna ended up telling me that she had ten kids total, and that she wasn't able to raise any of them. She doesn't go into detail, but it sounds like they were all either raised by the State or by other family members. She sounds very proud of the fact that even though she didn't raise them, she's still in touch with all of them and is currently living in a house with her granddaughter, Jocelyn, and Jocelyn's kids. She's very straightforward about it. I actually need to grab a piece of paper as she gives me the names of all my siblings.

There were four different dads and ten kids. I think I got it right.

Father - Pedro Martinez
Kids - Pete, Jesus (me!) and José (Lee)
Father - Bernard Hill
Kids - Bernard Jr. (Pookan), Darwin (Duke), Willina, and Linda
Father - Albert Legg
Kids - Albert Jr., Christina, and Gigi

She starts listing grandkids and I have to stop her. I just found out I have seven new siblings, as well as this brother Pete who is still missing. And a mom. That's a lot to process.

Unfortunately, one of Donna's kids, Duke, died a few years ago from heart problems, although it also sounds like maybe he was shot or something at some point, and it's hard to tell what his cause of death really was, but it doesn't really matter. Donna starts crying when she tells me about it, and I start feeling upset, too, knowing I wouldn't get to meet him, but the truth is that I am so overwhelmed that I am crying about everything.

After a couple of hours, we hang up and I call Rosa and Lee, waking them up. I tell them all about it and then Rosa starts crying and Lee gets kind of quiet. I realize I haven't even told John about it yet, so that's what I'll do when

Bio family—Taken in Philideliphia at the party. Starting Back Left: Kim (sister-in-law, Dwaine's wife), Honey (sister-in-law, Albert's wife), Albert (brother), Jesse, Willina (sister), Gigi (sister), Lee (brother), Linda (sister), Christine (sister), Front: Michael (brother-in-law, Christine's husband), Donna (bio mother)

he gets up. I have no idea how I'm going to sleep tonight. Donna told me she will call me again in the morning. She has a lot to process, too.

For the next several days my phone starts ringing at 6:30 a.m. Donna doesn't seem to care that there is a three-hour time difference. Not only am I talking to Donna, but the calls start coming in from my siblings. Our conversations are a mix of giddy laughing, tears, and telling each other about our lives.

I call Christopher and tell him my news, and he and his mom agree to give me a few days off. They also agree that I need to fly to Philly to meet this new family of mine. Lee is getting calls as well, and he and Rosa are trying to find the cash to make the trip, too. I think Lee mentioned that his biker gang, The Free Souls, would be loaning him the money. I'm curious if the gang knows that Lee is going to visit his new Black relatives.

I called my dad to let him know about finding Donna. He wasn't exactly excited about it, but he tried his best to be supportive. He let me go on for a while, but then asked why Lee wasn't returning his calls, as if this situation is somehow related. I reminded him that he and Lee haven't been talking for some time, and suggested maybe he call to apologize to Lee. Lee thinks my dad is only interested in having him pick up some booze to bring to his retirement community. I can't believe my dad is acting like everything is normal, but in a way it's kind of grounding.

So far, I have talked to all of my new siblings except Bernard Jr., also known as Pooken. Donna let me know that he is in jail, and will probably end up being in prison for a long time. He will actually have a hearing when we are in Philly, and she thinks maybe we can meet him either in the courthouse, or during visiting hours. Pooken is Jocelyn's dad, the granddaughter that Donna lives with right now. He sounds a lot like Lee, and I guess if there is a silver lining to his situation, it is that the family isn't going to be judgemental regarding all the time Lee spent in prison. I'm not sure what Lee has told Donna yet, so I try to make sure that I don't share anything that isn't mine to share.

"You know, son, it just breaks my heart that you and Joe had such a hard time in foster care. I left my home when I was a teenager because my Daddy kept touching me in ways I didn't like. Do you understand what I'm telling you son? I told my mom what was happening, but she didn't want to believe it, so I just started running away. After a while, I ended up going to this place called Hillcrest Home for Girls. It's in Salem, down the road from the Home for the Feeble Minded. I hated it there at first. It was on a farm and they gave us all different jobs. I ended up getting used to it, but it was a tough situation."

I try not to gasp. Or cry. I end up telling her about Dammasch and Merle and she gets choked up. Maybe I shouldn't have told her. I mean, I don't want her to feel guilty, but I am shocked at some of the things we have in common. In some ways, it is humbling to hear about Donna's life. She told me that she grew up in Port Orford, Oregon, and that they didn't have a floor in their house. Or running water. They had an outhouse for a bathroom. She told me they used a wood stove for heat and an ice box for a refrigerator. She and her brother and sister would work in the woods picking ferns, huckleberry bush, and chisholm bark, selling the first two things for decorations and the last to use as a laxative.

Donna lived at Hillcrest until she turned 17, when they gave her a bus ticket to Portland. She told me she ended up living in an SRO downtown, and that she met my father, Pedro Martinez, on Burnside Street. She was 18 years old when her first child, Pete, was born.

"I thought I had tuna fish poisoning. I didn't know anything about sex, nothing about how things worked when I was growing up. I found it all out on my own. Nobody told me. I'd eaten some tuna fish out of a can. Pedro, I called him Pete, went down to get Mama-san, we were in a hotel, and she was the hotel matron. Well, Mama-san come up to see me. She said, 'Oh … you have a baby, baby.' I knew I was getting big, but I could still wear all my clothes. So we went to St. Vincent's hospital and I had Pete."

I asked her about my father, and she told me that he was killed in a bar fight sometime after Lee was born.

"He was a boxer, and they were drinking, and they were having a fight and he got killed. He got hit and he died. I'm sorry you never got to meet him."

I'm not sure how I feel about that. Like Duke, it's another loss of someone I don't know, yet is still connected to me on some level. It's so surreal to hear about Donna living in Old Town. That was where I was living when I was downtown. That area has been the poor "Skid Row" area for such a long time, full of drugs and heavy drinking. I know she was there 20 years before I was there, but somehow knowing we were running the same streets helps me feel connected.

I asked Donna if she had been working as a prostitute, and she was very offended. I tried to back pedal and apologize, letting her know I had been given that information as a kid. I also tried to tell her I didn't think it was a big deal. In fact, it would have been one more thing we had in common.

She is really vague about some details, and I'm not sure if that is due to her memory issues, or if she's still a little shy about what she shares. She doesn't really seem to have a filter, and swears like a sailor, which feels very different from my mom and dad, but very familiar and similar to Lee.

When Donna saw a photo of Lee on Facebook, she burst into tears and she said, "If you had used that photo to try to add me as a friend, I would have immediately accepted."

The two of them look really similar, and I am trying to ignore this nagging feeling, I'm not sure what it is. It doesn't really feel like jealousy, but just one more situation where my sense of belonging isn't as clear as I would like it. As if Lee's physical resemblance to this woman I just met is one more thing that I don't have for myself. Donna doesn't have a photo of my dad and I wonder if I would feel more connected to him if she did.

The first sibling from Philly I really feel connected to is Albert. It wasn't immediate, and I could tell that he was a little suspicious of me at first. Albert and his sister Christina actually called me that first morning, as Donna had started calling all of the other kids in the middle of the night to tell them the news. Both of them have been calling me on their own, but for some reason Albert and I have had the deepest conversations.

Albert is married to a woman named Doneen, that everyone calls Honey, and they have five kids. He has worked for Boeing for over 30 years, and he kept asking me about my own experience working for Boeing. Obviously this was pretty confusing because I haven't worked for Boeing a day in my life.

He told me he had been hearing about these missing boys—Jesse, Joe and Pete—his whole life, and that Donna had a photo of three boys on her bedroom wall that she told him were these missing boys.

The boys in the photo were older than we were when we were adopted, and they looked much more Native American than me and Lee. She also told Albert that she had

Donna Bearheart Hurst, bio mother

seen us as adults, that we were living in Seattle, and that we worked for Boeing.

I didn't know what to say. Once we realized that I had nothing to do with that story, he explained that his relationship with Donna was strained, and I think that in some ways we started bonding right then and there. It felt like the first sibling who trusted me enough to tell me that there were some dynamics that were pretty dysfunctional, as if I couldn't figure that out on my own.

I promised him I would never lie to him, and that I had only talked to Donna the day before. He laughed and said that if he actually thought about the dates, that Donna's stories about drinking in bars with her long lost sons in Seattle didn't really make sense.

Albert told me that over the years, he had his own resentments against Donna, but not against his siblings. He wanted me to know that he felt the same way about me and Lee, and he couldn't wait to meet me in person. I thought I even heard his voice break, but I'm not sure. I'm not used to having straight men share their emotions. It's definitely not something Lee can do. Or my dad. Albert told me that his own dad was killed, and I told him that I lost my adopted mom and my sister, and I know it's not the same as someone you love being killed, but I think we bonded over that, too.

John is being supportive, but I can tell he's nervous because he's smoking more than usual and nervously cooking even more than normal. He's not planning to go with me to Philly yet, and he keeps asking me to be careful. I'm planning to go a day before Lee and Rosa. Something tells me I need to make sure it's all OK before they arrive. I'm nervous about the whole racial thing with Lee, but I'm also nervous these folks are going to be OK, and we won't end up getting hurt either. I don't really know what going a day early will do, but at this point everyone is cool with the plan, so it's happening this way. I find a Quality Inn near the airport that Albert says is clean and safe, and he has agreed to meet me there when I arrive. Now I just need to figure out how to go through the motions of my job, pack for Philly, and somehow stop my head from spinning so I can get some sleep.

Chapter 14

Mom-Donna

It's an overcast day when I land in Philly, and I am glad I brought my favorite bomber jacket. I forget about seasons sometimes after living in Palm Springs for so long. Instead of the classic four seasons, we have "Comfortable Perfection," "The Snow Birds Arrive," and "Unbearable Hellscape."

It's October, and while everyone else in the world is glued to the news about the presidental election, it's the furthest thing from my mind. I grab my bag, and make my way to the rental car company. Albert offered to give me rides while I'm here, but I really need my own wheels in case I need to make a fast getaway. I am kidding. I think. Maybe not.

As I drive up to the Quality Inn, I see Albert and Honey standing in front of the hotel lobby. Albert's smoking a cigarette, which is a relief to see. I didn't want to worry about my smoking offending anyone, because God knows I'm going to be needing my nicotine fix on this trip. My heart's beating pretty fast, but I'm trying to look cool and not break into a sprint to get to him. A big smile crosses his face and he yells out, "Hey Big Brother!" *Oh my God, I love this guy already.* We both hold out our arms for a hug, and I think I see Honey taking our picture.

We're going to my mom's house, but first Albert and Honey want to take me by their house to introduce me to their kids. Honey's mom lives with them too, and I'm up for anything. I quickly check into my room, splash some water on my face, change my shirt, and take a deep breath. *You've got this, Jesse.*

Albert lives in a lovely house and his kids are just adorable. He has four grown sons, and one daughter and they are all out of high school. They all stand up to shake my hand, and are really polite. Albert introduces me as their uncle, and they immediately refer to me as Uncle Jesse. I try to make sure I have all their names right—Albert Jr. (Albee), Brandon, Danny, Iona, and Andre. I know I'm going to meet a lot of people this weekend, and I know I can't remember all of them, but this feels important. Honey's mother is sweet, too. Really, the whole family is as lovely as can be. I brought some of my mom's costume jewelry with me to give to the women in the family, and Honey's mom is just gushing about the brooch I picked out for her. She immediately puts it on the lapel of her sweater and keeps looking down at it and smiling.

I ask Albert if we should get going to see Donna, and he assures me we won't be late for anything this weekend. The rest of the family laughs at that, and I just smile. Albert takes me to meet all his neighbors, introducing me as "My Long Lost Big Brother."

The neighbors are all very friendly and welcoming, but I am just struck by the look on Albert's face. He's beaming. I can't remember another time when I had that effect on someone else. Has John even beamed about me? Has Lee? Maybe my parents did when I was young and cute and they first brought us home. I have to believe they did at some point in my life.

Albert lets me know that I might be a little shocked when I see where Donna has been living. I let him know that I've seen a lot in my life, and that it would be hard to shock me. Unfortunately, though, he's right, and as we get deeper into North Philly I have to admit that I'm totally blown away. I haven't seen streets like these in real life before. The houses are like row houses, crammed together side by side without any kind of yard or green space. The streets are tight and filled with kids running around everywhere. I'm not seeing any white faces, and I wonder if my eyes are big because Albert looks at me and laughs, "Like I said, it's different over here."

We pull up in front of Donna's home and I hate to say it's the worst street in the neighborhood, but it's the worst street in the neighborhood. I take another deep breath. Part of me wants to run inside, yelling "I'm Here! I'm Here!" and another part of me feels like I need to smoke a whole pack of cigarettes. I'm relieved when Albert asks if I mind if we smoke one before going in. It hasn't occurred to me that he might be nervous too.

The door is opened by three kids, who are staring at us with big eyes. The oldest one turns around and yells, "They're here!"

The small hallway feels like it is filled with people immediately, but I realize it's just us and all these children. Albert introduces me to the kids, and they reach out their hand to shake mine. A young woman comes down the stairs. This is Jocelyn, their mother. Albert reminds me that Jocelyn is Pooken's daughter, and he lets me know that Jocelyn is legally deaf but can read some lips. I hold out my arms for a hug and she shyly gives me a squeeze.

The house is crammed with furniture, piles of laundry, and people. I look down the hall into the kitchen and see my mother sitting at the table. She's smoking a cigarette and she has her phone on the table. I make my way into the small room.

"Hi, Donna!"

"Oh, hi."

I'm immediately disappointed and floored by her indifference.

I ask if I can give her a hug.

"Well sure you can, son. It's nice to finally see you."

She doesn't get up, so I lean down and we awkwardly embrace. I have to be honest, it's not what I was expecting. She's definitely not beaming, and if anything she seems a little put off to the whole experience. Maybe she's overwhelmed. I'm definitely overwhelmed. The other people there are all talking at once and the kids are starting to bicker and I'm trying to have this moment I've waited for forever and part of me wants to yell at everyone to shut up and the other part wants to close my eyes and be back in Palm Springs. There is another part that just wants to crawl under the table with this woman and ask if this is finally really happening. I ask if I can sit, and she gestures toward the chair across from her.

I remember that I brought the jewelry to hand out, and ask if she would like to pick something out. She shrugs, looks at it for a minute, and tells me that I can pick something for her. I find a necklace with matching earrings that I think will compliment her style, which I'm not really clear about, but I say it anyway. I mean, she's 82 years old, but she definitely isn't dressed in the same conservative manner of my mother.

I try to make a big deal out of telling her it's the best quality of all the items I have to offer. She thanks me, but then shows me the necklace she is wearing. It contains a tiny amount of Duke's ashes. I can't compete with that, and then tell myself how dumb I am for thinking in those terms. I try not to react, as I spy the cockroaches scurrying around the kitchen floor. It reminds me of my days living in the SROs in downtown Portland. I guess I assumed she would be in a more comfortable place by now.

We talk for about an hour, and I tell her that Lee and Rosa are flying in tomorrow. I ask if she would like to stay in my hotel room with me, as there are two beds, and I feel like it might be easier than having to drive to this part of town before picking them up at the airport.

"Well, OK son. That might be nice. I can't remember the last time I stayed in a hotel."

Jocelyn agrees to pack a bag for her, and Albert looks a little shocked that I'm making this suggestion. I'm kind of shocked at myself, but I feel like it might help us really spend some time together. Maybe my years of being a caregiver are showing, because when Jocelyn packs some Depends in her bag, I don't flinch.

I can definitely sense some tension between Albert and Donna in the car on the way to the hotel. I try to make small talk and ask about Jocelyn's kids, life in Philly in general, and the plans for the party that Albert is throwing us. He tells us that he's got the whole thing covered, and that we should just plan on showing up the day after tomorrow in the early afternoon. Honey tells us that she and her mom have been cooking for days, and I think I see Donna roll her eyes. OK. That makes a little more sense, I guess. She's got pride. After being in both Donna and Albert's houses, it makes sense why Albert is hosting the big get together, but I understand that might sting for her.

I'm trying to figure out what I should call her. "Donna" seems too casual, like we're pals or something. "Mom" doesn't feel right either. Not yet. In my head I'm calling her "Mom Donna" because my own mother is the person I call "Mom." So far I've gotten away with not calling her anything to her face. Maybe I should calm down and realize I'm only four hours into this thing, and that some of this stuff will work itself out.

We all have a cigarette outside the hotel room. I carry

Donna's bag in, and she immediately chooses the bed closest to the bathroom. She looks around, and even though
I warned her that it wasn't fancy, I think she's a little disappointed. We end up watching TV and ordering a pizza.
That night I try to sleep, but between Donna's snoring and
my racing mind, it's really difficult. There's a time difference
too, so I give up on any plan on sleeping. I slip out of my
room around 2 a.m. and call John. He's trying to be sweet
and is acting like he's interested in hearing about all these
new people. He lets me go on and on, and then quietly asks
if I'm OK. I take a breath in between puffs on my cigarette.

"I'm OK. My head is swimming, but I'm glad I'm here.
It's a lot. But I'm OK."

I can't decide if I will feel more relaxed with Lee and
Rosa here, or if that will make it worse. I decide that it will
be better, and that I can't worry about them. I go back to
the room and somehow manage to drift off for a bit before
Donna wakes me up to ask me where she can get a cup of
coffee.

I'm not sure who suggested it, but once Lee and Rosa
were in the car with me and Mom Donna (I'm going to try
this name out), we decided we should go to a bar. I'm not
going to say we "needed" to go to a bar, because that just
makes us sound like alcoholics, but we definitely needed to
go somewhere and just sit and talk, and if alcohol would
help take the edge off, well that was a bonus. We found
an Irish Pub not far from the airport, and we piled into a
booth, with Donna and Lee sitting next to each other. I
have to say, the resemblance was uncanny. Rosa and I just
kept looking back and forth and then at each other and
shaking our heads.

I admit that I was a little nervous about Lee's rough
edges, but to be honest, Mom Donna seemed more com-

Donna and Lee with their one finger salute

fortable around him. It was as if his rough edges helped put her to ease. Rosa is a social worker who inspects nursing homes, and is used to talking to older people she doesn't know. Even though I know she's still really depressed, she has rallied for this trip, and is even more chatty than I am, and so that helped us all start talking. We held up our glasses of beer and made a little toast, and at one point Rosa pulled out her phone to take a photo. Lee rolled his eyes and said, "Oh here we go!"

He and Donna looked at each other and said something obscene and then both of them looked right at the camera and flipped the bird, cackling together. They both have their long hair back in a ponytail, and besides Lee's goatee and knuckle tattoos, they look really similar. The expression on both of their faces is one of joy, and I'm so relieved that Lee didn't experience the same reception that I had from Donna. I'm telling myself that it's because I spent this time with her and she's more comfortable, but I think that anyone who looked at the two of them could instantly tell they are related. I don't say this out loud, but I wonder deep down if maybe Lee's dad is different from my own.

Lee and Rosa have a room in the same motel, and we decide to go back and hang out the rest of the day. We all have a cigarette outside before getting in the car and my mom's eyes light up when I hand over four packs of smokes that I bought for her at the bar.

My sister Christina and her husband Mike have driven down from New York, and they plan on coming by the hotel to meet us. Christina is Albert's younger sister and is the person that I've had the most contact with on the phone besides Albert and my mom. Donna warns us that Christina's husband may try to talk to us about religion, and we all agree that he might have a hard sell in this crowd. We also agree to be polite. I'm so relieved when I meet Christina that she's enthusiastic about meeting us, immediately running up to me and Lee and giving us hugs.

"Hey Big Brothers! Oh my gosh, this is exciting!"

She talks a mile a minute, and she immediately starts teasing Donna about these handsome men she's been hiding from the rest of us. At one point she asks us where her husband Mike and Rosa are, and we realize they are in Lee's room. When I go knock on the door, Rosa gives me a look that says "Oh, thank God," as Mike has been preaching the gospel. I don't have a sense about him yet to know if it's something I can tease him about. Albert has been texting me all day about the party, and about how it's going, and he even stopped by briefly to meet Lee, who everyone is calling "Joe," which is short for José. He kept shaking his head and looking back and forth between Lee and Donna, just like everyone else.

Mom Donna has been telling us about how she met each of the men who are fathers to her kids. She met her first child's dad, Pedro, on Burnside street in Portland when she was a teenager. She tells us that she left Baby Pete with someone in the SRO while she was out working. She's very vague about it, but I think that's when he was removed from her care. Next thing she's talking about is being in Klamath Falls, Oregon, staying with Pedro's family. She tells me that Pedro, my dad, had a brother named Jesus, who I may be named after. She had Lee, "José," and somehow the two of us ended up at the Boys and Girls Aid Society. I try to remember what I learned from staying with Louann—stop paying attention to the dates and the details and listen to the stories. I also wonder again if Lee and I actually have the same dad. I pass for white most of the time, but of the two of us, I am the one who really looks like I have some Latin blood. Lee has always been blonde. I definitely don't bring this up. I wonder if, when we find Pete, he and I will look alike. I guess I won't be the oldest anymore.

We hear about how she met Bernard Hill, who was Pooken and Duke's dad. He was in the Air Force and was wearing a nice jacket. Donna told us they were in a bar where a fight broke out. Donna's shirt was ripped in the bustle of the chaos, and he gave her his jacket. The next time she saw him in that same bar, he came up to her and reminded her that she had his jacket. It doesn't seem like that smooth of a line to me, but apparently it worked, because she ended up staying with him for some time. She tells us she knew her family wouldn't let her come home with babies from a Black man, so she ended up following him north to Seattle, where she had Linda. They eventually made their way to Philly, but the couple separated when Donna was pregnant with Willina. Again, she doesn't tell us who ended up raising those kids.

Mom Donna met Albert Legg, who is Albert, Christina, and Gigi's dad. "He was OK, but he just kept going to jail," she says.

Albert tells us that he and his sisters spent time in foster care, as well as with family, but were always raised to not have hard feelings toward his mom. He also tells us it's been Pooken who has been the one to keep all the siblings together, even when they were living in different homes.

The last man on the list is Tony Taylor. That's Kia's dad. Mom Donna didn't give birth to Kia, but she ended up taking care of her. I think Tony is the one who helped her buy her house, and she was with him even though, as she put it, "he got all sick and cranky."

I tell Donna that I found the title to her house on Bosnall Street. She tells us that it's a couple of blocks from where she's staying now, but unfortunately it was destroyed in a fire. She tells us she still owns the property, but no one is banging down her door to buy an empty lot in North

Philly, so she thought it would make the most sense to move in with Jocelyn.

We all take turns going outside to smoke and we're shaking our heads at these crazy stories. Even though we don't say it out loud, there is an unspoken agreement to not push Donna into telling us why she gave us up, or why her other kids grew up in other homes besides hers. Instead, we focus on how proud she is of still being considered their mom, and as long as she has someone to pay attention to her stories, she is not shy. We also haven't asked her what she did to look for us, or about this fake photo of her missing kids.

That night, I realize that although it's still a little odd to be sharing a room with this woman I have just met, I am exhausted and fall off to sleep. I didn't realize how much tension my body had been holding, wondering how this was all going to go down. I think I was so busy worrying about the ways that it could be awful, that I'm starting to realize the ways this is actually pretty amazing. While it's not the instant connection I felt with Louann, and it's not the lifetime of mothering I had from my adopted mom, this is something different. I haven't quite settled into it yet, and neither has she, but it's feeling better. Definitely better than what it was like to be searching. I think.

Chapter 15

Brothers

It's the day of the party, and I am sensing some tension coming off of all of us. Lee snapped at me, Rosa rolled her eyes behind his back, and Mom Donna was being a little demanding. She's complaining that Jocelyn didn't pack her things correctly. I resist the urge to remind her that she could have packed her own bag, but I decide to go outside and call John while I have a cigarette. I start by complaining about everyone.

"Are you feeling tense too?"

"Of course I'm feeling tense! This whole situation is crazy, but it isn't going to help anything if we're all snapping at each other. I'm just trying to support everyone so this will go well."

"Right. But who's supporting you?"

"Well, that's why I'm calling you. You're supposed to do that. Just tell me to relax, I've got this, everyone is going to love me."

"Relax. You got this. Everyone is going to love you."

"Now was that so hard?"

This is how our conversations go. I don't remember if we were ever more romantic or mushy with each other, but I suspect lots of old married couples are this way. It's calming though, and it's a chance for me to get out of that room to clear my head for a second.

I've got some concerns about Mom Donna's hygiene, from the point of view of a caregiver, but when I brought it up with my new sister. Christina, she just started laughing and saying, "That's on you Big Brother! She might not like that, but go ahead and bring it up with her. Knock yourself out!" I don't think that's the best plan.

As we turn the corner to Albert's house, I can see that the whole block is already filled with cars. I agree to drop Mom Donna off in front so she won't have to walk. There are already people on the porch, and even though we are on time, I'm worried maybe Albert will think we are late. I remember his line about not being late during this trip and I try to not worry about it.

When we walk in, I am shocked at all the people inside. Albert immediately comes up and yells, "Here they are! These are my big brothers!" and we are immediately surrounded by people coming up to introduce themselves. Honey hands me a soda and asks if I need a beer instead and I am grateful because there are so many people shaking

Donna and Lee surrounded by bio nieces and nephews, and grand nieces and nephews

my hand and telling me their names that I won't remember, and there are some hugs, and it's really overwhelming. Albert's family is there, and so are all my siblings and their friends and families. There are people who are cousins and grandkids and friends and the stream is constant.

I look over at Lee and he's surrounded too. I realize that he and Rosa and I are the only white faces in the crowd. I take a breath because I know that's probably really uncomfortable for Lee, but I can't worry about him. I think to myself that this is probably what it's like for most people of color, to be outnumbered by people who don't look like you do. The fact that we are being treated like celebrities in this scenario is where the parallel ends.

The party lasts for hours, and the steady stream of people doesn't really slow down. I am handed drinks and plates of food. Honey's mom is wearing her brooch on her dress, which is sweet. Mom Donna is sitting outside smoking. I notice that she's really only talking to people who come up to her, almost as if she is receiving them or something. She looks uncomfortable, but isn't quite as worried about impressing everyone like us.

Lee is telling people about motorcycles and he and Kia are hitting it off. Kia isn't Mom Donna's biological child, but is the daughter of the last man she was involved with romantically, and Kia calls her Mom. Lee has brought pendants from his motorcycle club to hand out, and she accepts them for her kids and tells him she will hold onto them so her kids don't lose them. Lee starts creating games with the kids and Rosa is passing out candy. I had planned to put some space between me and Lee, because I was worried that he might slip up and accidentally say something offensive. I didn't need to. Lee is on his best behavior, and is drinking beer, and being charming and making everyone laugh. I'm so proud of him.

At one point, someone suggests we take a group photo. Donna is sitting in a chair and Christina's husband is kneeling down next to her. The rest of us are crowded around with our arms around each other trying to fit into the frame. We are clear that Duke is missing, and so is Pooken. I'm still the tallest one, even among all these new people. We're all chattering about having the picture taken on our own phones and I swear we took about ten different photos. The one I have has most of the people smiling, but when I really look at it I see Mom Donna has the most serious expression of all of us. Maybe she was tired or just overwhelmed. Or maybe this is what pride looks like?

Albert tells me he was counting people at the party, and at one point he lost count at 350 people. Obviously, his house isn't that big to host that many people, so there were folks spilled out onto porches and his yard. A lot of folks were coming and going. I am having a great time, and am feeling overwhelmed, but not because I'm nervous. It's because I can't believe that I'm related to all these people. Talk about joining a tribe. I try to give myself a break about not remembering names, because there's just no way.

Unfortunately, the next thing I know, Rosa is telling me that Christina just accused her of flirting with Mike, and brought up that it was inappropriate that she and Mike were alone together that day they met in Rosa's hotel room. Rosa told her that she was being polite to Mike as he talked to her about God, and that Christina is being ridiculous. At some point Christina told Rosa to "fuck off" and now Rosa is telling me she needs to leave before she goes off. I'm pretty confused, but before I can react to that situation, Mom Donna comes up and tells me she's leaving because she and my sister Gigi are fighting and she just told Gigi to get the fuck away from her. I try to ask what's going on, and Mom Donna says, "Get the car, Jesse, we're leaving." My head is spinning and so I find Albert to tell him we need to leave.

"Brother, don't worry about it. This is what happens. It's not about you."

I decide that instead of getting into it and helping everyone get along, I'd just load up Donna and Rosa and take them back to the hotel. My head is swimming in confusion, and even though I didn't want to leave, I think that maybe having a little space isn't a horrible thing. I sent John some texts and included the photo with all my siblings. He texted the emoji that is supposed to mean "OMG." When he asked how it went, I replied that it was a lot to process. I never understood the expression about falling asleep before your head hits the pillow, but that's what happened that night. I was utterly exhausted.

It's two days since the party, and we are headed to the courthouse. Pooken has his arraignment for a burglary charge, and I'm driving Lee, Mom Donna, and Jocelyn. Mom Donna keeps talking about how I need to talk to his attorney to ask if we can tell him about me and Lee, and to make sure this attorney is a good one. She keeps telling me I need to check him out. I'm not sure what his options will be if I don't think he's good, and I don't know how I would determine if he's good or not. If anything, Lee's the one who should be trying to figure that out since he has more experience being in the courtroom than I do. I guess the fact that Lee spent 22 years in prison is evidence that he didn't have great attorneys, so maybe it's my job after all.

We find the courtroom and while we're waiting for Pooken to be brought in, I ask to talk to his attorney. I tell him that we are his client's long lost adopted brothers and ask if we can have some time to meet him privately. The attorney seems pretty moved by the story and promises to talk to the judge to see if he can arrange a visit after the hearing. He somehow gets this information to the judge, even though the courtroom is full of other people who are there for their own arraignments. I guess that's what's going on anyway. The judge instructs us that we can come up to the bar, but we can't cross it. We can't have any physical contact with Pooken. We must wait until we are told that we have permission, and she tells us we will be given three minutes to introduce ourselves. We smile and nod and agree to all of it.

Pooken is finally led into the courtroom and he sees Donna and Jocelyn. He then sees us and seems to know something is up.

The Judge asks for complete silence in the courtroom.

"Mr. Hill, it has come to our attention that your two brothers are here in the courtroom today, and that you have not met yet. I told them that they may approach the bench and they may introduce themselves to you. They have been instructed that they have three minutes to do this and you are not to have any physical contact with them. Do you understand, Mr. Hill?"

Pooken is nodding his head and his eyes are wide and Lee and I make our way to the bench. The courtroom is so quiet you can hear a pin drop. The tension feels as thick as fog.

"Hey Pooken! I'm Jesse and this is Lee. We were named Jesus and José, and we've been looking for Donna our whole lives."

Pooken's eyes fill with tears, and we talk for a few minutes, telling him where we live and how we found Donna. The rest of the court remains silent, except I hear a few sniffles. I look back at Donna and Jocelyn, and the people sitting behind them are crying. Even though Pooken has tears in his eyes, he also has a huge smile on his face.

The Judge lets us know that our time is up and tells us to return to our seats. For the rest of the procedure, Pooken keeps turning around to look at us and he has a big smile, even though he's not getting out of jail anytime soon. Unfortunately, he's been in and out of prison for years, and the Judge has remanded him to jail without any chance for bail. He is taking it seriously, but obviously we're causing a big distraction.

After the procedure, I am waiting to talk to his attorney in the hall. He's let me know that he is trying to scramble together a visit for us to see Pooken in jail before we leave town. We are standing there when other people from the courtroom start to come up to us.

"You know, this was an awful experience today because our son was arrested. But you all really made this special. Thank you."

"Good luck to you all and God Bless You."

"Thank you for making this horrible day a little bit better."

"You all are cool. Congrats for finding your family."

None of us really know what to say. I admit that although I am thrilled to meet my brother, I am also pretty excited to be part of this whole *Perry Mason* courtroom drama. For once, Lee and I are on the right side of the bar, and we both agree that it feels like a scene out of a movie.

I ask Lee if he's uncomfortable being back in a courtroom and he just shrugs. He keeps asking Jocelyn about Pooken's charges, but it's not clear if she's being realistic or pessimistic. Albert warned us that Pooken will probably be sent away for a while because of his history. Albert has also commented a few times how much Lee reminds him of Pooken. It's meant as a compliment, as Albert really loves Pooken, and visits him more than any of his other siblings. I think it's also Albert's way of letting Lee know he is OK. Albert has said that when Pooken isn't locked up, he's the one trying to keep the siblings together. I figure it's because he's been the oldest one, until now.

When we finally do get to see Pooken in a visit room, we are given extra time because we are coming from out of state. They even let us give him hugs and talk face to face, not with one of those phone things behind plexiglass.

Pooken is focused on us and is trying to downplay his situation. He even apologizes that this is how we have to meet, but we assure him that we don't have any judgment. He keeps smiling and shaking his head, which we're getting used to now, especially when people see Donna and Lee side by side. There's no question we're related and he keeps thanking us for coming. I tell him that I will write to him and will put money on his account. We exchange addresses, and more hugs, and he is taken back to his cell.

On our final day in Philly, I drive to Albert's to say good-bye to his family. Honey's mom answers the door wearing the brooch on her big, fluffy bathrobe. Albert's kids have come over to give hugs. They call me "Unc" now, which I love. We agree that Albert will meet us at a restaurant out by the airport for breakfast. We've got to take Mom Donna home first. I tell all of them that I can't wait to come back to Philly to visit.

As we are dropping off Mom Donna, she and Rosa are chattering about future visits. Rosa is trying to get her to come to Portland, and is letting her know they even have a guest room. We are all smoking, and we're giving hugs to Jocelyn and her kids too.

Mom Donna starts us off. "Well shit. This has been something, hasn't it?"

I give Mom Donna a long hug, and it's definitely less awkward than when we met a week ago. I promise to come back as soon as I can get time off work. We all pile into the car to meet Albert for breakfast.

We meet Albert and chat about everything that has happened over the last several days, all of us shaking our heads. He reassures us that all the drama at the party will die down, and that in some ways it's pretty tame compared to some of the other times the whole family gets together.

"You all are in it now!"

He insists on paying for our meal. Albert is wiping his eyes before we even hit the parking lot. We turn to give him a hug and he just starts telling us how much he's loved meeting us.

"Please don't go away again. Please promise me that you're not going to go back to the West Coast and forget about us."

Lee and I both go in for a hug at the same time, and what do you know, but all three of us are bawling like babies. We're all promising to stay in touch, and I keep telling Albert that I didn't go to all this trouble to find him, just to forget about him. I even take off my bomber jacket and hand it to him, letting him know it's my favorite, and that this is his way of knowing I will be back to claim it. Albert is talking about losing Duke and missing Pooken, and now that he knows us, he loves us, and he just can't bear for us to disappear. We all cling to each other for what seems like forever, but it is only a few minutes. We break apart and start wiping our eyes, laughing awkwardly at the display of emotion. I think it's Lee that says something about how *God dammit, there must be something in his eyes,* and we laugh even more. Rosa is crying, and then she takes a photo. Here we are, Lee, Albert, and me, arms around each other, smiling at the camera. Brothers. Family.

Afterward

On the third day of my second trip to Philly, things got weird. I was in Mom Donna's room, installing the flat screen TV I had bought for her bedroom. Jocelyn's kids are gone now, and they have guys in here instead as renters. It's not completely clear if the kids are at their dad's or at a foster home, but I know DHS is involved, and I know Jocelyn's pissed. I don't know what happened exactly. I sent her money to buy beds for all five of them, but Mom Donna told me she spent it all at the strip bar, which Mom Donna calls the "Jiggly Butts Bar." Of course, I don't say this out loud, but when I first returned to Palm Springs from Philly, I informed John that I thought we should have Jocelyn's kids live with us. All five of them! Of course John had some concerns about that plan. Now that they're gone somewhere, I think that maybe I wasn't so crazy after all.

While I was trying to install the TV, I heard yelling. There's a lot of yelling here, but when I went out into the tiny living room, I saw this guy that's living in one of the kid's rooms and he's yelling at Jocelyn and Mom Donna, really getting into their faces. I guess he hasn't paid his rent yet, and I don't really have time to get the full story about who is right or who is wrong. I'm at least a foot taller than this guy, and he's currently threatening an 80 year old woman, so I march in and get in his face and tell him to calm the hell down.

Well, he started going in on me, telling me to mind my own fucking business and who is this white faggot anyway, when I see Mom Donna turn around and beeline into her room. I'm thinking, at least she's backing down. Maybe this will blow over. Maybe she's more level headed than I thought. Next thing I know, she is coming back into the room and she's got a taser in one hand, and an ice pick in the other! She starts charging at all of us while she's yelling and swearing up a storm. I look at this guy and say, "God dammit, if I get tased, I'm going to be pissed!"

Luckily, he backed down and went up to his room, yelling the whole time about these crazy bitches this and fucking bullshit that. And then he left.

I tried to hide the shaking in my hands when I lit a cigarette on the front porch of her house. All the neighbors were already out on their porches, looking over to see what the racket was about. These row houses are all smashed together on this narrow street, so everyone can hear everything. I know I can be a real drama queen back on the West Coast, but this is some next level drama, and I have to admit, I am wondering what I have gotten myself into with these people. The neighbors look curious but not shocked. Down here on Mom Donna's block this is pretty normal. I guess that's why her neighborhood is called The Badlands. I guess that's why I can expect to get pulled over again by the cops as I drive back to my hotel. They keep asking me what a white guy is doing in these parts, driving a rental car. They assume I'm just here to buy drugs. I tell them I am visiting my mother, and they laugh. When I give them her name and address and tell them I just found her after 59 years, that lends some credibility, with one of them even saying, "Now that's a story!" I still get angry though, and I guess I understand what it feels like to be racially profiled or something. Mom Donna and the rest of the Philly family just think it's funny.

Tomorrow I am going to try to visit Pooken. He is sending me letters about once a week these days. Each one starts in the same way:

"By the time you receive my letter I truly hope and pray

it finds you in the very best of Health–Physically, Mentally, as well as Emotionally and your spirits are lifted so very highly."

The writing is cursive, with really neat penmanship, and when Pookan writes a small i he uses a heart as the dot. He also uses a heart for the letter o and at the bottom of question marks. He writes the letters in pen, mostly, and colors the hearts red. Sometimes there will be a card, purchased from the commissary, and often there will be a drawing that includes more hearts, with the names of all of our brothers and sisters. Every once in a while he will use colored pencils, alternating colors for paragraphs or even lines of writing. It must have taken him a long time, but time is what Pooken has now. Anyone else might assume these were love letters written by a middle school girl. I don't mean that as an insult at all. It's really sweet when you realize it's from a guy who's not getting out of prison anytime soon. God knows Lee didn't write me letters that were this affectionate when he was in prison. But then again, he didn't need to. He knew I would do anything for him. I have been putting money on the books for Pooken, and he's really thankful. Usually there is an ask within the letters, mostly about me helping him find a female pen pal. I ignore that part, but I always write him back, at least when he hasn't gotten himself stuck in the hole.

I keep gravitating toward Albert's house. Mom Donna likes that we are bonding as brothers, but she still makes comments about how I have my head up Albert's ass. I know it bothers her, because he's the one out of all of her kids that has the least to do with her. He has had a job for 30 years with Boeing, and he has a house, and he and Honey have sent all their kids to private school. I don't think that makes him stuck up. I think that makes him stable. Plus, he's the one who really reaches out to me and Lee, calling us all the time when we're back on the West Coast. He doesn't seem to need or want anything from us except our love. This is all so overwhelming and exciting, and if someone would have told me that I would be in a house in Philly trying to avoid being tased by an 80 year old woman who happened to give birth to me, I would have told them they were high. I just keep breathing in and shaking my head, taking it all in. My hands were shaking less as I lit that next cigarette.

I don't know this yet, but on March 23, 2021, I will call Donna to wish her a happy birthday. We'll talk for a bit, and I will wonder if she has already started drinking to celebrate, because she sounds a little off. I tell her I love her, and wish her a happy birthday. I will get a call four hours later from my sister Gigi letting me know that Jocelyn found Mom Donna dead on her kitchen floor. She had a massive stroke. I don't know this yet, but I will follow Mom Donna's wishes and I will make all of the funeral arrangements, flying back to Philly for her funeral and cremation. A few weeks later, I will drive up to Crescent City, meeting Lee and Rosa and my Aunt Louann, and we will spread Mom Donna's ashes on the nearby reservation. I will follow her instructions and will spread them in the four directions, with Louann guiding me. We will choose a gorgeous spot in the Redwoods, 1,000 feet from the ocean, and we will take a video for the Philly kids. It will be incredibly peaceful.

I don't know this yet, but when Mom Donna dies, I will grieve, but it will be complicated. I will feel sad, but I will also feel something surprising. My dad will have died a year earlier, and now I will be in the world without any parents. There will be no one left I need to impress or expectations to live up to. There will be no one whose love I feel obligated to earn.

For the first time in my life, I will actually feel free.

John and Jesse on a cruise, 2012

Jesse's Acknowledgements

I would like to thank Keri Ault, for all her hard work in writing this book. This project would not have gotten off the ground without her putting pen to paper and making it happen. She's the best, and yes, Keri wrote that part. I would also like to thank the folks at Anamcara Press for recognizing the potential in my story and bringing this book to life.

I would also like to thank my family. Louann Adamson was the first biological family member I found on this journey, and I will always appreciate her openness and support. I would like to thank all of my biological siblings who were willing to be interviewed for this project. I would like to thank my brother, Lee Scott, who has always stuck by me no matter what was happening. He's the original Ride or Die. I would like to thank Lee's lovely wife Rosa for sticking with my brother, keeping him on the straight and narrow, and always offering her support when things got bumpy.

Finally, I would like to thank my partner, John Wilson, who has been a great support and has stood by me through this whole journey. He was along for the ride in finding my biological family as well as my work in writing this book.

Keri's Acknowledgements

I would like to first thank Jesse Scott for having such an interesting life! Your openness and sense of humor throughout this process has been humbling. You are one of the most resilient people I know.

I would like to thank all my fellow writers who spent countless hours reading early versions of this project. Cassie, Alison, Ed, Joe, and my mom Marilynn, you guys are the best. Thank you, Brian Benson, who finally convinced me to write in first person. I would like to thank the lovely folks at Anamcara Press for believing in this project.

Most of all, I would like to thank Jeff, Landon, and Fisher. You all have my heart forever and ever.

About The Author

Jesse Scott is former case manager for people living with HIV, former caregiver, and is currently living out his retirement in the deserts of the West Coast. He continues to surprise people who have known him for years, for still being alive and kicking.

About The Writer

Keri Ault is a social worker living in Portland, Oregon. Her writing has appeared in the Meadowlark Reader, You Might Need to Hear This, Cirque, and Proof That I Exist. When she is not writing or working, she is trying to spend as much time outside as possible, even when it's raining.

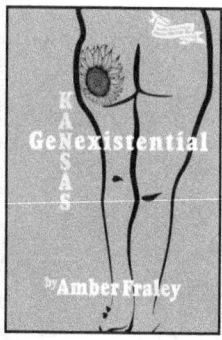